The Capture of Black Bart

More Remarkable Lives for Middle-Grade Readers

— • —

Alexandra the Great: The Story of the Record-Breaking Filly Who Ruled the Racetrack

Becoming Emily: The Life of Emily Dickinson (February 2019)

The Big, Bold, Adventurous Life of Lavinia Warren

A Girl Called Vincent: The Life of Poet Edna St. Vincent Millay

Krysia: A Polish Girl's Stolen Childhood During World War II

THE CAPTURE OF
BLACK BART

~~~~~~~~~~~~~~~~~~~~

Gentleman Bandit of the Old West

NORMAN H. FINKELSTEIN

CHICAGO
REVIEW
PRESS

Library of Congress Cataloging-in-Publication Data
Names: Finkelstein, Norman H., author.
Title: The capture of Black Bart : gentleman bandit of the Old West / Norman
    H. Finkelstein.
Other titles: Black Bart, gentleman bandit of the Old West
Description: Chicago, Illinois : Chicago Review Press Incorporated, [2019] |
    Includes bibliographical references and index. | Audience: Ages 10 and up.
Identifiers: LCCN 2018014940 (print) | LCCN 2018015235 (ebook) | ISBN
    9781613739969 (adobe pdf) | ISBN 9781613739983 (epub) | ISBN 9781613739976
    (kindle) | ISBN 9781613739952 (cloth)
Subjects: LCSH: Brigands and robbers—California—Biography—Juvenile
    literature. | Outlaws—California—Biography—Juvenile literature. |
    Stagecoach robberies—California—History—Juvenile literature. | Frontier
    and pioneer life—California—Juvenile literature.
Classification: LCC F866.B59 (ebook) | LCC F866.B59 F55b 2019 (print) | DDC
    979.4/04092 [B] —dc23
LC record available at https://lccn.loc.gov/2018014940

Interior design: Sarah Olson
Map design: Chris Erichsen

Printed in the United States of America
5 4 3 2 1

For Tova, Joseph, and Iliana

CONTENTS

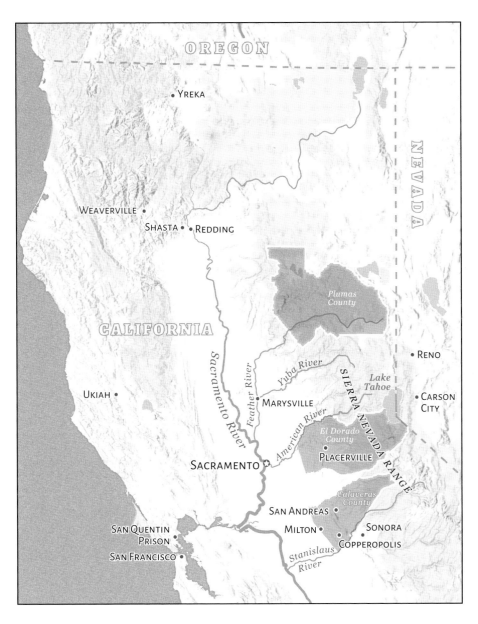

Black Bart's stagecoach holdups spread all over the rugged land-scape of Northern California. Lawmen wondered how he could travel long distances on foot so quickly between robberies. Only with his capture was the truth revealed.

1

A GHOST APPEARS

---

*I don't want your money, only the
express box and mail.*

—BLACK BART

Before automobiles, telephones, and airplanes, stagecoaches linked the isolated mining towns of the Old West. While passengers bounced and swayed inside drafty, dusty coaches, valuables were stowed under the driver's seat in a sturdy green wooden box of Wells, Fargo & Company. The box was encircled by an iron strap and secured with a heavy padlock. The box weighed 25 pounds when empty. People called it the "treasure box" for all the wealth it contained.

Robbers set their sights on those distinctive green boxes. Many thieves were chased off, wounded, or even killed by drivers or guards. Those who escaped were relentlessly tracked down by James B. Hume, Wells Fargo's chief detective, a fearless but fair former sheriff. His job was to chase down anyone foolish enough to rob a Wells Fargo stagecoach. He always lived up to the company's motto—"Wells Fargo never forgets." Jim Hume was very busy. In 1875 alone, Wells Fargo stagecoaches were stopped 34 times by robbers, with a total of $87,000 (worth nearly $2 million today) stolen.

On July 26, 1875, driver John Shine slowly guided his stagecoach up Funk Hill, a steep mountain road near Copperopolis, California. He knew this part of the trip from Sonora to Milton, California, was especially hard on the horses. Without warning, a ghostlike figure jumped out from behind a large boulder in front of the huffing horses and blocked the stagecoach's path. Shine brought the horses to a quick stop. The figure crouched low, using the horses as a shield. Menacingly, he aimed a double-barreled shotgun at the driver.

Shine stared at the strange-looking figure before him. The bandit wore a long white duster (a type of lightweight coat), and his shoes were wrapped in rags. Only his eyes were visible through two holes cut out of the flour sack that covered his face. Comically, a dark derby, or bowler, hat sat on his head, placed at a jaunty angle.

TOUGH HANK MONK

Stagecoach drivers like John Shine were a tough group. They had to be strong, resourceful, and in command. Perhaps the best known and respected among them was Henry James "Hank" Monk. Mark Twain, in his book *Roughing It*, humorously—and with a bit of exaggeration—related the time when Monk drove the stage carrying famed New York newspaper editor Horace Greeley, who coined the phrase "Go West, young man":

Horace Greeley went over this road once. When he was leaving Carson City he told the driver, Hank Monk, that he had an engagement to lecture at Placerville and was very anxious to go through quick. Hank Monk cracked his whip and started off at an awful pace. The coach bounced up and down in such a terrific way that it jolted the buttons all off of Horace's coat, and

continued on next page . . .

Legendary driver Hank Monk and his stagecoach.

finally shot his head clean through the roof of the stage, and then he yelled at Hank Monk and begged him to go easier—said he warn't in as much of a hurry as he was awhile ago. But Hank Monk said, "Keep your seat, Horace, and I'll get you there on time!"—and you bet he did, too, what was left of him!

"Please throw down the box," the robber politely ordered in a booming voice. As Shine reached beneath his seat to struggle with the heavy box at his feet, the

The Wells Fargo treasure box.

bandit turned slightly and shouted toward the boulders above, "If he makes a move, give him a volley, boys." Shine glanced upward and caught sight of gun barrels aimed at the stagecoach from behind the boulders. Unarmed and concerned with the safety of the passengers aboard, the driver had no choice. Down went the green Wells Fargo express box and a canvas United States Mail sack.

Inside the coach, one of the passengers drew his gun and prepared to shoot at the masked robber. Another warned him to put the gun away. "Do you want to get us all killed?" he asked. When one frightened passenger threw her purse out the stagecoach window, the robber picked it up and handed it back. "No, Ma'am," he graciously said. "I don't want your money, only the express box and mail." Then he yelled toward the driver, "That will be about all, boys. Hurry along now and good luck to you." As the stagecoach moved forward, Shine observed the robber on the ground working to open the express box with a hatchet.

Almost at once, the robber was surprised by a second stagecoach lumbering up the hill. With the hatchet in one hand he raised the shotgun toward driver Donald McLean, who brought the stage to a stop. "Please throw down the box," the robber shouted. But this coach did not carry an express box, so the masked robber allowed it to go on its way as he continued to hack away at the box on the ground.

Shine drove the stage a short distance uphill and stopped. McLean's coach arrived within minutes. Looking around to make sure the robber was not nearby, Shine dropped to the ground. Slowly and carefully, he inched his way on foot back down the road to retrieve the empty express box. As he neared the site of the holdup he looked up. The gun barrels were still there and pointing directly at him. Shine held his breath, expecting bullets to fly. When nothing happened, he moved forward step-by-step and made a startling discovery. There were no hidden bandits. The "guns" were just sticks made to look like gun barrels. Shine picked up the now empty box and mail sack, returned to his stagecoach, and rushed on to Copperopolis to seek help.

The local Wells Fargo agent telegraphed Sheriff Benjamin Thorn of Calaveras County and Wells Fargo detective James B. Hume, who eventually arrived with a posse, a group of armed men organized by the sheriff. There were no tracks to follow and only one clue. Hume noticed that the mail sack was slashed open in an

A traveling stagecoach scene.

unusual way, forming an upside-down letter T. There wasn't much money taken from the now empty express box, but that didn't matter to Hume, who posted this notice when he returned to town:

> REWARD! **Wells, Fargo & Co.'s express box containing $160 in gold notes, was robbed this morning.... $250 and one–fourth of any money recovered, will be paid for the arrest and conviction of the robber.**

No trace of the robber was found. This was Jim Hume's first contact with him. It would not be the last.

Wells Fargo reward poster after the July 26, 1875, robbery.

2

WELLS FARGO CONNECTS THE WEST

Wells Fargo has come! Wells Fargo has come!
—CHARLES T. BLAKE

GOLD! In 1848, newspapers headlined the discovery of gold in California. Stories of people "picking gold out of the earth" captivated readers. From big cities and small villages all over the world, thousands of adventurers set out from their small farms and shops for California. A popular melody of the time, "Oh, Susanna," expressed the excitement:

I soon shall be in 'Frisco,
And then I'll look all around,
And when I see the gold lumps there
I'll pick 'em off the ground:
I'll scrape the mountains clean, my boys,
I'll drain the rivers dry.
A pocket-full of rocks bring home,—
So brothers, don't you cry.
Oh, California!
That's the land for me.
I'm bound for San Francisco,
With my wash-bowl on my knee.

Reaching California was not easy. Some prospectors traveled west across the prairie and desert, fighting danger, hunger, and thirst. Others took long ship voyages around South America. Some got off ships on Panama's Atlantic coast and trudged through insect-infested rain forests to reach the Pacific, where they boarded other ships for San Francisco. Each came with a personal dream of fame and fortune. Crew members even abandoned their ships to join them. Despite the fervor and optimism, few struck it rich.

Before the gold rush, California had a population of less than 160,000, nearly all Native Americans. Following the massive influx of settlers, the nonnative population grew from less than 1,000 to more than 100,000 two years later. The United States acquired the California Territory from Mexico in 1848 after the Mexican-American War. Because of the newly discovered gold and exploding population, California was quickly admitted into the Union, becoming the 31st state in 1850.

Once arriving in San Francisco, the adventurers found adobe houses and canvas tent villages along with dance halls and barrooms, and swindlers and shopkeepers sold food and tools at raised prices. Newcomers

Gold rushers in the Bay of Panama converting canoes into schooners to take them north to California.

GOLD SEEKERS ADVISE, STAY HOME!

The journey to California was long and hard. For those going by ship through Panama there was often a long wait there to get to San Francisco. One traveler wrote home in May 1849: "I am still here, waiting patiently for the return of the steamer *California*, which has now been due three or four weeks. . . . It is calculated that there are now 1500 Americans on the Isthmus . . . waiting to procure a passage up the coast. Many are getting discouraged, and almost everyday witnesses the return of more or less of them on their way to the States."

Those traveling by land across the Plains lived through other hardships. One gold rusher wrote, "After the period of six months . . . we have crossed the mountain of difficulties, and the desert of starvation." Then, based on his experiences, he left a clear message: "If any have the gold fever, tell them to come any other way under heaven than this."

Another traveler, Jacob S. Crum, wrote more forcefully, "I hope there are none of my friends who really desire to come to this land of fiction.... I advise all to stay at home, if they can, as it won't pay to come to this country."

Miners at work on the banks of the Stanislaus River.

soon noticed the absence of women and children. One new arrival described his temporary sleeping arrangements on bales of hay shared with "two real judges, five ex-governors, three lawyers, and as many doctors, streaked with blacksmiths, tinkers and tailors."

After providing themselves with necessary supplies, they made their way to the mining camps that sprang up along streams and riverbeds of the gold regions, mainly along the Sacramento River and in the foothills of the Sierra Nevada. It took luck rather than skill to find gold.

Miners panning for gold in California.

An observer described the process: "The miner stoops down by the stream, choosing a place where there is the least current, and dipping a quantity of water into the pan with the dirt, stirs it about." After much careful stirring and the addition of more water, the amount of gravel and dirt decreased, leaving behind the heavier gold particles. It required lots of hard work to collect varying amounts of gold. The miners were resourceful. As the gold became harder to find, they developed more sophisticated methods. When gold seemed to dry up in one location, miners moved to another.

Gold miners worked in remote areas. They feared leaving their diggings—the piece of land where they worked—since others could rush in while they were gone to claim their plots. They could not just leave their accumulated gold dust and nuggets lying around. They needed a trusted and secure way to transport their gold down the mountains and to the cities below.

There were several express services that delivered mail and packages throughout the eastern United States. The largest was the American Express Company, founded in 1850 by the merger of three smaller express firms owned by Henry Wells, William G. Fargo, and John Warren Butterfield. With news of the California gold rush, Wells and Fargo wanted to expand American Express's business to California. When the company's

Sutter's Mill, a sawmill in Coloma, California, where the
California gold rush began.

Henry Wells (left) (1804–1878) and William Fargo (1818–1881) helped create the American Express Company in New York. In 1852 they formed the company bearing their names, which served the West.

board of directors vetoed their idea, both men formed their own separate company and "launched in 1852 an industry that began the development of the Great West."

Wells, Fargo & Company began express operations in California to ship packages, purchase and sell gold, and transport passengers. They opened offices throughout the gold mining areas and offered a variety of services. They installed secure safes in their offices and charged miners for taking care of their gold dust. Armed messengers to the remotest gold camps provided reliable service that miners trusted. A Wells Fargo receipt for gold was a solid guarantee that the company would pay for a lost or stolen shipment. An 1857 Wells Fargo newspaper advertisement stated, "Freight, Parcels, Money and Letters, forwarded and delivered with dispatch, and at reasonable rates. . . . Personal attention of the Messenger is given to all matter entrusted to our charge."

Miners were cut off from their families and loved ones. Letters were the only means of keeping in touch, and mail service was irregular. In June 1851, there were only 34 US post offices throughout California, few in the gold diggings. Wells Fargo filled the gap by delivering mail to nearly every town and mining camp. The miners tended to move often, in search of better diggings, and the post office had no way of following them. But Wells Fargo agents did. One newspaper reported, "It seems that private enterprise is ahead of Uncle Sam."

People trusted Wells Fargo, and it gained a reputation of honesty. The company taught its agents, "The most polite and gentlemanly treatment of all customers, however insignificant their business, is insisted upon. Proper respect must be shown to all—let them be men, women or children, rich or poor, white or black, and it must not be forgotten that the company is dependent on these same people for its business."

The arrival of a Wells Fargo stagecoach or wagon in town created a sense of expectation. Was there a

Where the railroad ended, Wells Fargo stagecoaches began their journeys to the remotest mining camps and towns throughout the West.

friend or relative on board? Was there a package to be delivered? Composer Meredith Willson described that excitement in his song "The Wells Fargo Wagon" in his popular musical play *The Music Man*:

> *O-ho the Wells Fargo Wagon is a-comin'*
>   *down the street,*
> *Oh please let it be for me!*
> *O-ho the Wells Fargo Wagon is a-comin'*
>   *down the street,*
> *I wish, I wish I knew what it could be!*

From its earliest days, Wells Fargo's coaches competed with other express companies in the West, creating a network of scheduled routes carrying people, packages, gold, money, and mail. By 1866, "Wells Fargo combined all the major western stage lines . . . and rolled over 3,000 miles of territory, from California to Nebraska, and from Colorado into the mining regions of Montana and Idaho." The company set up a series of relay stations, or "stages," along their routes to exchange fresh horses and provide meals for passengers. That word—*stage*—soon gave the stagecoach its shortened name. Those stations, usually not more than a small adobe hut and a corral, were usually arranged every 10 to 12 miles. Passengers had a few moments

Stagecoach leaving the Wells Fargo office in Virginia City, Nevada.

to stretch their legs while the horses were changed. Larger stations for longer journeys were located about 50 miles apart; passengers could receive meals and overnight lodging.

The coaches were built by the Abbot-Downing Company of Concord, New Hampshire. The usual

Stagecoach accidents were frequent. The routes stagecoaches traveled were in no way related to today's paved highways. Along narrow mountain cliffs, over dusty plains, and across swollen rivers, stagecoach drivers worked hard to keep their passengers safe.

configuration included three inside bench seats for nine passengers. Additional passengers sat outside on top. Most coaches were shipped by sea from Concord to California, a journey of over 19,000 miles around

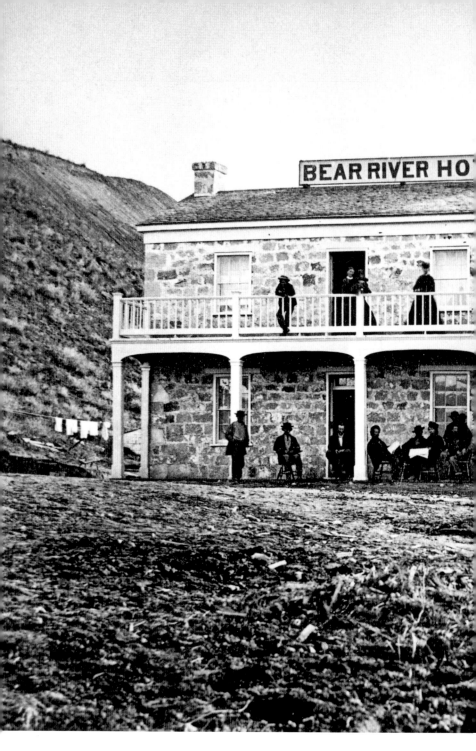

Wells Fargo stage stops were located everywhere.

A HARD TRIP

———•———

Stagecoach journeys were difficult, but passengers still appreciated a mode of travel that operated on a schedule, was fast and efficient, and delivered them safely (most of the time) to their destinations.

Yet, getting a good meal during such journeys was not easy. Hungry passengers were limited to whatever food was available at the relay stations. Mark Twain described one meal in a stagecoach station:

The station-keeper up-ended a disk of last week's bread, of the shape and size of an old-time cheese, and carved some slabs which were as good as . . . pavement, and tenderer. He sliced off a piece of bacon for each man, but only the experienced old hands made out to eat it, for it was condemned army bacon which the United States would not feed to its soldiers in the forts, and the stage company had bought it cheap for the sustenance of their passengers and employes [*sic*]. . . . Then he poured for us a beverage which he called *Slumgullion* and it is hard to think he was not inspired when he named it. It really pretended to be tea, but there was too much dish-rag, and sand, and old bacon-rind in it to deceive the intelligent traveler. He had no sugar and no milk—not even a spoon to stir the ingredients with. We could not eat the bread or the meat, nor drink the *slumgullion*.

Cape Horn in South America. The Concord coach was specially constructed to overcome the rough terrain of the West. It weighed over 2,200 pounds and was built to last. Instead of the usual steel springs, it swung on a thorough brace, "a stout leather strap attached to C-springs front and rear, on which the body of the vehicle" was suspended.

The coaches were not only durable but also were sights to behold. Drawn by six horses, the brightly colored coaches, usually red or green, had doors decorated with scenic artwork. Prominently displayed above the door on each side was the name WELLS, FARGO & CO. One writer described the arrival of a Wells Fargo coach in a mining camp: "If there is a prettier street picture of animation than a red Concord coach with six spirited horses in harness and a good reinsman on the box, we have not seen it."

Though a Wells Fargo stagecoach in motion was a striking sight indeed, what went on inside the coach was a different matter. Passengers endured many discomforts and were often "crowded together as

Concord coaches on a train on their way west. The coaches of the Abbot-Downing Company of Concord, New Hampshire, were considered the finest available. Each coach seated nine passengers inside and six outside.

the needs of the hour and the size of the passengers demanded, to sit elbow to elbow, side by side to the journey's end." They were jolted by rocks and ruts on the ground, while dust and rain easily passed through the poorly curtained open windows. "Passengers, dozing in corners or curled up on the middle seat, would fall in a heap at a sudden lurch, untangle themselves, and doze off again."

Those seeking gold without having to wield a pick and shovel soon realized that under the stagecoach driver's seat was the Wells Fargo treasure box. The

STAGECOACH TRAVEL TIPS AND ETIQUETTE

In 1877, the *Omaha Herald* published these hints for stagecoach travelers:

☞ The best seat inside a stagecoach is the one next to the driver. . . . You will get less than half the bumps and jars than on any other seat. When any old "sly Eph," who traveled thousands of miles on coaches, offers through sympathy to exchange his back or middle seat with you, don't do it.

☞ Never ride in cold weather with tight boots or shoes, nor close-fitting gloves. Bathe your feet before starting in cold water, and wear loose overshoes and gloves two or three sizes too large.

☞ When the driver asks you to get off and walk, do it without grumbling. He will not request it unless absolutely necessary. If a team runs away, sit still and take your chances; if you jump, nine times out of ten you will be hurt.

☞ In very cold weather, abstain entirely from liquor while on the road; a man will freeze twice as quick while under its influence.

☞ Don't growl at food stations; stage companies generally provide the best they can get.

☞ Don't keep the stage waiting; many a virtuous man has lost his character by so doing.

☞ Don't smoke a strong pipe inside especially early in the morning. Spit on the leeward side of the coach. If you have anything to take in a bottle, pass it around; a man who drinks by himself in such a case is lost to all human feeling. Provide stimulants before starting; ranch whisky is not always nectar.

☞ Don't swear, nor lop over on your neighbor when sleeping. Don't ask

continued on next page . . .

how far it is to the next station until you get there.

☞ Never attempt to fire a gun or pistol while on the road, it may frighten the team; and the careless handling and cocking of the weapon makes nervous people nervous. Don't discuss politics or religion, nor point out places on the road where horrible murders have been committed.

☞ Don't linger too long at the pewter wash basin at the station. Don't grease your hair before starting or dust will stick there in sufficient quantities to make a respectable "tater" patch. Tie a silk handkerchief around your neck to keep out dust and prevent sunburns. A little glycerin is good in case of chapped hands. Don't imagine for a moment you are going on a picnic; expect annoyance, discomfort and some hardships. If you are disappointed, thank heaven.

sturdy boxes were made of pine, oak, and iron and when loaded with gold bullion, cash, and legal papers could weigh between 100 and 150 pounds. Why work hard when all you had to do to get rich was rob a stagecoach? Soon, stagecoach robberies became common experiences for drivers and passengers. Wells Fargo responded by hiring armed messengers to "ride shotgun" next to the driver. They were "the kind of men you can depend on if you get into a fix." The work was dangerous. Before becoming a famous writer, Bret Harte worked as a Wells Fargo messenger sometimes known as an expressman. He explained, "Stage robbers were plentiful. My predecessor in the position had been shot through the arm, and my successor was killed." As the number of stagecoach routes increased, many trips went without shotgun messengers.

Stage robberies were so common, one newspaper said they "were hardly worth noticing." Wells Fargo disagreed. In a 14-year period, between 1870 and 1884, Wells Fargo recorded 313 stage robberies. Four drivers, two shotgun messengers, and four passengers were killed. The total loss for these robberies was $415,000. The company paid out that amount to the people who had entrusted robbed valuables to its care.

To show just how seriously the company took these holdups, it spent over $500,000 to track down and

A STAGECOACH DRIVER'S SKILL

In his short story "An Ingenue of the Sierras," Bret Harte described fictional stage driver Yuba Bill's skill in avoiding a holdup:

The huge vehicle swayed from side to side, rolled, dipped, and plunged, but Bill kept the track, as if, in the whispered words of the Expressman he could "feel and smell" the road he could no longer see. We knew that at times we hung perilously over the edge of slopes that eventually dropped a thousand feet sheer to the tops of the sugar-pines below, but we knew that Bill knew it also. The half visible heads of the horses, drawn wedgewise together by the tightened reins, appeared to cleave the darkness like a ploughshare, held between his rigid hands.

prosecute the robbers. Stage robbing was not a secure profession. Five of the robbers were killed during holdup attempts, another 14 were hanged by citizens, and 240 were convicted in the courts and sentenced to prison.

The robbers, sometimes referred to as highwaymen or road agents, differed in style. Some left the passengers alone and focused only on Wells Fargo's treasure box. Others showed no compassion for travelers. On July 10, 1864, two armed highwaymen stopped the stage bound for San Jose, California. While one ordered the driver to throw down the box, the other aimed his pistol at the passengers and demanded, "Come out with your money, men." When one passenger turned over what he claimed was all he had—$2.50—the bandit replied, "You have no business to travel on this road without more money." Yet, when the driver requested that the robbers return any letters they found in the box, the robbers readily agreed. The driver then shared a drink of whiskey from his flask with them before the robbers allowed the stage to proceed. Not all robberies ended so peacefully.

When a Wells Fargo stagecoach was robbed in June 1866 on a lonely road in Nevada County, California, a sheriff's posse quickly formed to track down the robbers. One lawman, Stephen Venard, soon encountered the robbers and the treasure box, containing $8,000 in gold dust. Killing all three robbers with four shots from his Henry rifle, he returned to Nevada City with the gold and his story. Wells Fargo presented him with a new gold-engraved Henry rifle and offered him a reward of $3,000, which he promptly shared with other members of the posse.

Another example was the unfortunate robber of the Shasta and Weaverville stage in October 1876. He "jumped from behind a bush, covering Wells Fargo's messenger, John McNemer, with a shotgun." The messenger had no choice but to throw down the treasure box. The robber grabbed the box and yelled to the driver to drive on. When the stage was out of sight, McNemer jumped off and ran back to where the robber sat opening the box. The messenger raised his shotgun and fired, killing the robber instantly.

And sometimes, robbers made mistakes. When three armed bandits stopped the La Porte, California, stage and told the driver, "We want the box," he replied, "Boys, I have not got a thing. I don't carry the box." After one of the robbers carefully searched the stage, he told the driver, "By God, I believe you." The thieves had stopped the wrong stage. When they discovered their error, one of them said, "There is honor in this crowd," and did not try to rob the driver or his passengers before letting the stage travel on.

Other robbers seemed to be amateurs. When two robbers stopped the Petaluma and Healdsburg stage, they ordered the driver, William Wood, to climb down from his seat quickly or he would "get the top of his head shot off." They made Wood hold his hands up while they searched his pockets and took $43, a watch, and a ring. Then they ordered the passengers out of the coach and relieved them of cash and watches. What the robbers somehow did not notice were the two heavily loaded Wells Fargo express boxes inside.

There seemed to be an unwritten code of honor between some drivers and robbers. When two other bandits stopped a San Jose–bound stage, the four passengers did not have much in cash or valuables to offer. Then, while the driver shared a drink with the robbers from his flask, a disappointed robber said, "You can go ahead, now; we will not trouble you anymore; it don't pay us to come here—you carry too poor a crowd."

As two robbers suddenly appeared in front of Hank Monk's stage, the surprised veteran driver lost control of the startled horses, which sped ahead of the equally surprised highwaymen. Once Monk brought the stage to a stop, the shotgun messenger called back to the robbers to come forward. Unsure whether they now faced a trap, the robbers turned tail and disappeared into the brush.

Wells Fargo appreciated the dangerous work of its stage drivers and messengers. When two road agents tried to rob a stagecoach near San Bernardino, California, the driver, Thomas Peters, refused to stop. The robbers shot at him and hit one of the horses, which, although badly wounded, continued on for another three and a half miles before dying. Peters was able to escape, carrying the passengers and treasure box to safety and alerting authorities. Sheriff's deputies captured both robbers the next day in a gunfight. Wells Fargo recognized Peter's bravery by presenting him with an engraved gold watch worth $300.

Robbers relied on the element of surprise to stop a stagecoach, giving the driver or shotgun messenger little opportunity to respond. One newspaper account of a stage robbery near Paso de Robles took the passengers to task for not taking action: "The passengers, eighteen in number, were not disturbed and did not disturb the robber. . . . Eighteen passengers stand in awe of one man. We do not understand it." When a passenger stood up to highwaymen on the Quincy and Oroville road, Wells Fargo recognized his bravery in saving the treasure box by presenting him with a valuable gold watch. "That's the way to do it," a newspaper said. "It needs something to stimulate passengers to make some show of resistance. Half of the land pirates are arrant cowards, and will run, as did this one, on the first show of opposition."

In all stage robberies, Wells Fargo drivers and shotgun messengers faced constant dangers. When the Shasta stage was stopped near Redding, the driver obeyed the order to throw down the treasure box. Messenger Buck Montgomery, sitting inside the coach, picked up his shotgun and fired, wounding one of the robbers. Another robber took aim at Montgomery and killed him. In the exchange of fire, the driver was badly wounded in the knee. He handed the horses' reins to the passenger sitting beside him, who was also wounded but able to guide the stage away to safety.

Wells Fargo instituted a generous reward system to help solve robberies. A typical announcement was placed in the *Petaluma Weekly Argus* newspaper on July 4, 1873. The company offered a reward of $1,500, as well as one-quarter of the amount recovered, for the arrest and conviction of the highwaymen who robbed their treasure box on the Downieville stage. The exact sum stolen was $2,681.

With continuous dangers to its passengers and treasure boxes, Wells Fargo created a company police department. Working with local law enforcement officers, their detectives pursued highwaymen and investigated thefts. Law enforcement back then was not

Wells Fargo's express department in the Parrott Building, San Francisco.

Wells Fargo also provided banking services in the same building.

scientific. Clues were often overlooked. With news of a stage holdup, law officers formed a posse and went chasing after the robbers without paying attention to details.

A new era in solving crime began, however, with the hiring of James B. Hume as Wells Fargo's chief detective.

~ 3 ~

JAMES B. HUME, LAWMAN

Wells Fargo never forgets.

—COMPANY SLOGAN

J ames B. Hume was 23 years old when he left home to seek adventure and gold in California. He was born in 1827 in upper New York State into a religious, hardworking farm family. While Jim loved the outdoors and the company of his nine brothers and sisters, his days were filled with rigorous chores and farm responsibilities. When not working, he enjoyed school and reading, especially newspapers. Sundays were devoted to church services.

James B. Hume used scientific methods to track down the West's most notorious robbers.

In 1836 the family moved to Indiana, where the farmland was better. Jim worked hard there, too, but as he grew older he began to feel confined by the rigid life imposed by his father. Reading about the California gold rush inspired him to leave the routine of farm life. In March 1850, accompanied by his older brother John and several friends, Jim left Indiana for a new life in California.

The trip took five months. They traveled overland by foot, wagon, and horse at a leisurely pace, arriving in California in August. The group separated, with Jim and John panning for gold along the American River. They were making a little money, but the work was hard, and they did not care for the rough-and-tumble lifestyle that surrounded them. They moved often, from one location to another. John wrote home that "there is no such thing as society" in the camps where they lived.

Gold miners crossing the plains to seek their fortune.

The brothers soon grew tired of prospecting and decided to try shopkeeping instead. They opened a small store in Placerville, California, supplying miners with tools, food, and other supplies. John, who had studied law back in Indiana, opened his own legal office in town, which soon became more rewarding to him, financially and personally, than mining or tending store. John went on to a long career as a lawyer, elected public official, and district attorney.

Meanwhile, Jim, still hopeful of striking it rich, formed a small group of friends and set out for more gold mining. For several years he toiled through drought, hard work, and difficult living conditions. But when his hopes did not materialize, he gave up his mining career in 1860. During his years in the area he had become well respected and participated in local politics. To support himself he accepted a position as Placerville's tax collector. Two years later, recognized for his performance in that role, he was appointed to several town positions. He was now the city's marshal, police chief, and street commissioner.

Jim's several jobs, although bearing impressive titles, proved to be more boring than exciting. His main duties involved catching unlicensed dogs and keeping the streets clean. When the city passed a rule requiring property owners to clean the streets in front of their homes, a local newspaper reported, "Mr. Hume intends to strictly enforce the ordinance, and it is to be hoped that all citizens will cheerfully co-operate with him doing so. He expects the residents of Main Street to commence their scraping and sweeping operations this fore-noon, and so give that thoroughfare a bright, clean face for Sunday morning."

The residents of Placerville were more than delighted with Hume's performance of his duties. A newspaper editor wrote, "Our city, under the administration of our able, efficient and energetic Marshal, James B. Hume, presents a fine appearance." In 1863, Hume was reelected to his positions with a wide margin over an opponent. A year later he was appointed undersheriff of El Dorado County, expanding his law enforcement experience, which led to his first encounter with stagecoach robbers.

On March 4, 1864, a few miles from Placerville at a spot on the road known as Bullion Bend, two stages were stopped by a gang of six heavily armed men claiming to be Confederate soldiers. Although California was far removed from the battlegrounds of the Civil War, the men declared, "We do not want anything of the passengers. All we want is Wells, Fargo and Company's treasure to assist us to recruit for the Confederate Army." Their escape did not go smoothly.

Placerville, El Dorado County, where Jim Hume served as sheriff. The gold mining areas were rough-and-tumble places at first. Placerville's original name was Hangtown, which was changed once the town became more respectable.

Cornered in a hotel room by two deputy sheriffs, the bandits began shooting. With bullets flying in all directions, one robber and one lawman were badly wounded while the other deputy was killed. The remaining robbers escaped.

Jim Hume was away from town at the time, but two months later several of the escaped bandits were caught. Jim questioned them intently until they confessed. With information they provided and his own investigation and witness interviews, he set out to track down the rest of the gang. Traveling on horseback over 160 miles to a location near San Jose, he found them at a meeting of Confederate sympathizers. Jim burst into the room, arrested them, and brought them back to Placerville to face trial.

The lessons he learned from that case about investigating clues and interviewing witnesses stayed with him. As undersheriff, he frequently led posses in search of robbers and murderers. In one 1867 incident, he and his men cornered armed bandits on the road. Jim commanded them to stop. When they began firing, one shot hit Jim's arm but did not cause serious injury. Jim ordered his men to return fire. When the smoke cleared, one robber was dead and a second surrendered. A third robber fled, but Jim tracked him down and escorted him to Placerville to stand trial.

In 1869, the people of El Dorado County elected Jim to be their sheriff. His duties were explained in a newspaper article: "In that capacity it was his duty to convict or dislodge all the criminals that infested the wiles of that country." Jim took pride in protecting the county. He used his investigative skills to solve serious crimes, including arson (setting fire to property) and murder. Another newspaper praised his ability in stopping a jailbreak by writing, "It was thwarted by one of the most vigilant officers and intelligent detectives in the State." Despite his good work as a law officer and his popularity, he lost the next election in 1871. That did not stop him from doing his job through March 1872, when the new sheriff took over.

On November 28, 1871, a single highwayman held up the stage between Georgetown and Greenwood and escaped with the Wells Fargo treasure box containing $1,000 worth of gold dust. As soon as he was notified, Sheriff Hume set out for the robbery site. He tracked the robber's trail as far as he could until it disappeared. Jim returned to Placerville and publicly announced that he could not find a single clue. This was just a trick to make the robber feel at ease. Privately, Jim sent telegrams to Wells Fargo agents throughout the area, alerting them to be on the lookout for the gold, which was unusually shaped and easily identifiable. It took a few months until a gold buyer in a nearby county realized that he had bought that exact gold. Jim sent a deputy, who discovered the name of the robber, James Watkins, and learned that he had fled to Nevada. Jim contacted Nevada officials, and Watkins was returned to El Dorado County, where he was put on trial and sentenced to jail. Jim's trick succeeded.

During the 22 years he lived in Placerville, including eight years as undersheriff and two as sheriff, Jim made many friends. He participated in local political and social affairs and was an elected officer in his Masonic lodge, a popular fraternal organization. But now it was time for him to move on. One newspaper wrote, "Rogues, after they came to understand and know of Hume, gave El Dorado county a wide berth. Hume is probably one of the best detectives on the Pacific coast. . . . He is a kind and obliging man, but a determined and resolute officer." On March 4, 1872, the residents of Placerville gathered to pay tribute to Jim Hume with speeches of thanks and the presentation of an expensive gold watch.

Wells Fargo was concerned with the rising number of stage holdups and the theft of money by its own employees. They were aware of Jim's law enforcement experience and successes and his long cooperation with Wells Fargo in tracking down stagecoach robbers.

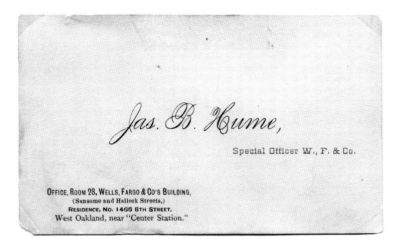

James B. Hume's Wells Fargo business card.

Wells Fargo offered him a unique position as their chief special officer. Although not clear from the title, he was hired to lead their own security department. At his job interview, Jim said, "I'll take the job but one thing must be understood: I am boss absolute." His employers happily agreed.

But before moving on to the Sacramento office of Wells Fargo, Jim took a year's detour to Nevada with the company's permission. The Nevada State Prison was experiencing embarrassing difficulties, including frequent prisoner escapes and one mass escape of 30 prisoners who killed guards and civilians as they fought recapture. The state needed someone competent to temporarily take charge and put the jail in order. Jim's reputation as an honest and proven lawman led the Nevada governor to appoint him acting warden of the prison. Once that job was completed, Jim began a legendary career with Wells Fargo that lasted over 25 years.

Over those years, Jim traveled throughout the West, protecting the interests of Wells Fargo, always remembering that "Wells Fargo never forgets." Building on his many law enforcement contacts, he set up a large force of cooperating investigators and paid informants throughout the area. He issued wanted posters and offered substantial rewards for the capture of criminals. Rule number 275 in the Wells Fargo instruction manual stated: "The Company offers a standing reward of $300 for the arrest and conviction of each person engaged in robbing the Express on the public highway, and will always aid in the prosecution of such criminals."

Newspapers reported his comings and goings but usually without details of who he was pursuing. His investigations were varied. During one stage holdup in 1871, the robbers buried the treasure box containing 60 ounces of gold dust. Three years later, Jim unearthed the gold and returned it to the company. Robbers also targeted the Wells Fargo offices. Jim investigated the robbery of the safe in the office of a Wells Fargo agent in Quincy, arrested the thieves, and recovered the stolen $800.

Sometimes, robbers just had no luck. When Jim investigated the December 4, 1875, robbery of the Caliente and Los Angeles stage, he uncovered a strange tale. After robbing the stage, the highwayman realized he did not bring along an ax to crack open the treasure box. As he carried the heavy box away, he fell into a ditch, breaking his foot and leg. He then crawled three-quarters of a mile to a mining camp, pushing the treasure box in front of him. There he found an ax and broke open the box. He fashioned a pair of crude crutches and stole a horse to escape.

But he did not count on Jim's keen powers of observation. When Jim showed up on the scene he made a useful discovery. The horse was fitted with a temporary shoe, which had left a distinctive trail and led to the arrest of the road agent.

It was not the only time that Jim used his tracking skills. Testifying in another case, he explained how he caught another stage robber: "I discovered two different boot tracks going in the direction of the robbery. I followed them almost continuously. . . . One was larger than the other. . . . They were very distinct and perfect." He then described the arrangement of the nail impressions and imperfections in the sole of the shoe. In front of the jury, he held the robber's shoe in his hand and pointed out the specific defects. Naturally, the court convicted the robber, who received a long sentence in California's San Quentin State Prison.

Jim Hume's interest in details solved many crimes. He became known for his skill in interrogating suspects "and getting them, through his persistent questioning to finally admit their guilt." He introduced the use of ballistics—the science of guns and bullets—to prove guilt. When three heavily armed robbers stopped the Yreka-to-Redding stage, the driver alerted the shotgun messenger who was riding in the coach. In an exchange of gunfire, the messenger killed one of the robbers. As the two remaining highwaymen quickly made their escape, they shot back wildly at the stagecoach, killing one of the horses.

As a posse formed to chase the robbers, Jim made a strange request. He ordered all the buckshot removed from the horse before it was buried or destroyed. During the trial that followed, Jim introduced the shot as evidence, comparing it with buckshot found in possession of one of the robbers when he was captured. For the jury, that was enough proof of the man's guilt, and he was sentenced to jail.

As time went on, Jim gained a reputation as an imaginative investigator. One newspaper said, "He is a terror to the jail-birds, and rascals, and always has an eye open for their special benefit." When a pair of robbers stopped the Bodie-to-Carson stage at 2:30 AM, the shotgun messenger killed one of them as the other escaped in the darkness with money from the treasure box. After the body was buried, Jim was notified and made his way to the crime scene. By then familiar with many known criminals, Jim dug up the body but did not recognize him. He did, however, find a bank book in the dead man's pocket listing the names of both robbers and a boardinghouse address in San Francisco. Keeping that information secret from the public so as not to warn the escapee, Jim notified the sheriff, who was able to arrest the surprised robber when he returned home. Case solved. A local newspaper commented, "J.B. Hume, the head of Wells, Fargo & Co.'s detective force, was especially sagacious [wise] in his plans for the detection of the surviving robber, and to his experienced judgement the success of the entire matter is mainly due."

Jim was a frequent visitor to San Quentin Prison as he delivered convicted robbers to serve jail sentences for their misdeeds. Back then, the prison was also a destination for sightseers, who arrived by boat from cities across San Francisco Bay. They enjoyed leisurely strolls in the sunshine by the water while gazing at prisoners locked behind barred windows.

Jim's friends particularly appreciated his good humor and took enjoyment from a newspaper article

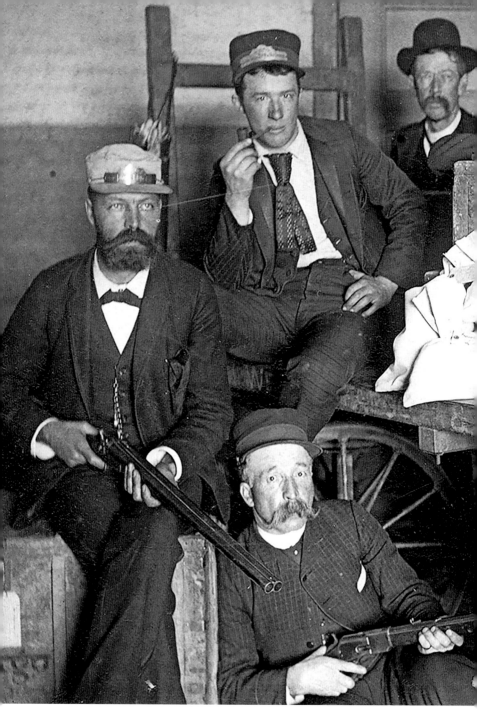

Wells Fargo stagecoach messengers posing with treasure boxes and shotguns. Shotgun messengers were a brave and hardy group. They were "the kind of men you can depend on if you get into a fix," according to their boss, Jim Hume.

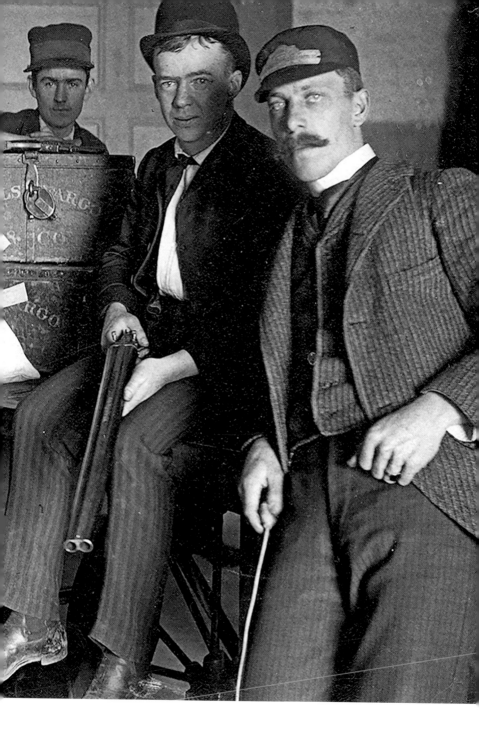

that described in detail his visit to the prison grounds with his future wife, Lida Munson: "As the steamer reached the wharf at San Quentin, a friend on shore recognized Hume, and called out to him, 'Halloa, Jim, is that you? . . . You do not seem to have anybody with [you] for the States' boarding house this trip.'" Hume laughingly responded, "Oh, yes, I have," and placed his hand on Lida.

She did not appreciate the joke, and later in the day, when the couple returned to their residences, she paid him back for publicly teasing her. As Jim left the streetcar to enter his hotel, Lida loudly shouted after him, "I do not think that man should ever have been pardoned: he should have stayed in prison every day of his term!" This joke did not stop the embarrassed Wells Fargo special agent from marrying Lida on April 28, 1884, at San Quentin in the home of his friend, the prison warden, Charles Aull, who once worked for Wells Fargo. A newspaper report on Jim's prison wedding remarked, "He doubtless is better pleased with this capture than any he has heretofore made."

James B. Hume created Wells Fargo's highly respected detective system, which relied on scientific evidence, cooperation with local sheriffs, and stubbornness to track down criminals. After the successful capture of a four-member gang of frequent stage robbers, a newspaper gave credit to the Wells Fargo "corps of officers, who under a careful and systematic detective campaign, in which neither money nor men have been spared," closed the case. "The present effort," the newspaper continued, "was one of the most systematic and determined that has ever been made upon any occasion upon the coast."

During his long career, Jim had many successes in bringing Wells Fargo stage robbers to justice. Yet, for a period of eight years beginning with the Funk Hill robbery in 1875, one highwayman eluded capture and challenged Jim's patience and reputation.

4

A LEGEND GROWS

And if there's money in that box,
tis munny for my purse.

—BLACK BART

Within a two-week period, driver Mike Hogan's stage between North San Juan and Marysville was held up twice. Each time, the objective was the Wells Fargo treasure box. During the first robbery, on December 16, 1875, a bandit wearing a checked shirt aimed a rifle at Hogan and gruffly shouted, "Hold up your hands or I'll blow your brains out." The robber, a heavyset man with dark hair and dark complexion, did nothing to hide his identity. He then ordered the driver to "hand out that box, and be quick about it." Hogan obeyed and asked if he could then move on.

The bandit responded, "Drive on or I'll blow your brains out." Hogan said he could identify the robber "without the least doubt" once he was captured.

The next holdup, on December 28, was different. This time the robber was covered in a white duster and carried a double-barreled shotgun. He jumped out from the side of the road and crouched in front of the lead horses for protection. Then in a loud voice he firmly but politely asked the driver to "throw down the box!" Hogan thought he saw a second gun barrel pointed at

Stage carrying mail, express, and passengers on the road.

him from the bushes and quickly obeyed the robber's instructions.

When a posse returned to the scene later, they discovered the smashed box and the US Mail bag cut open in the shape of an upside-down letter T. A newspaper reported that with this second robbery Hogan was "probably getting mad. Two robberies in as many weeks is more than he can bear, especially as he is an active and experienced police officer." Left behind was the fake "gun" fashioned out of a stick. Jim Hume realized

this was the same highwayman who had robbed the stage at Funk Hill on July 26. "This job is the work of a professional," he declared.

This bandit was not the only one on Jim Hume's list of Wells Fargo stagecoach robbers. Just a few days later, with the help of Sheriff Thorn and other Wells Fargo officers, he broke up one of the worst holdup gangs in California. A newspaper reported that Jim was "showing the prisoners how hopeless was their case, and getting them through his persistent questioning to finally admit their guilt."

It took six months for the "professional" to strike again. On June 2, 1876, the stage from Roseburg, Oregon, to Yreka, California, was stopped and robbed by a man whose appearance and actions fit the description of that individual. This time, although he tried to escape by tiptoeing away to hide his tracks, he nonetheless left behind impressions of his boot, which had identifiable marks. The local sheriff came across a stranger near the robbery site whose boots seemed to match the tracks and arrested him. When Jim Hume arrived and more carefully checked the boots, he determined that the man was not the robber and had him released. The identity of the real bandit remained a mystery.

Still, Jim now had several clues about the robber. Masked and wearing a white duster, he had a deep voice, was polite, and carried a shotgun. What Jim lacked was a name to go with the clues. This changed with the road agent's fourth robbery on August 3, 1877, between Fort Ross and Duncans Mills. Masked, wearing a linen duster with rags wrapped around his legs, the robber, armed with a shotgun, stepped in front of the horses. The driver, Ash Wilkinson, promptly obeyed the order to "throw off the box." The passengers on board were not harmed. When lawmen arrived on the scene, they discovered the empty broken treasure box and a Wells Fargo receipt under a rock on a nearby tree stump. On the reverse of the paper was a poem. Each line was written in a different writing style. The poem read:

I've labored long and hard for bread
For honor and for riches
But on my corns too long you've tred
You fine haired Sons of Bitches.

Black Bart, the Po8 [poet]

To the bottom of the page, Bart added the following sentence:

Driver, give my respects to our friend, the other driver;
But I really had a notion to hang my old disguise hat on his weather eye.

A passenger-loaded stage fording a river. Stagecoach travel was difficult.

Perhaps the message indicated that authorities were powerless to stop him or that he actually knew to target the stage that carried the richest treasure box. Although no one yet knew the robber's real name, his signature linen duster and double-barreled shotgun now gave him a colorful identity and the beginnings of a popular myth that captured the public imagination.

Nearly a year passed before Black Bart's next robbery. On July 25, 1878, he stopped the Quincy-to-Oroville stage, high in the Sierra Nevada. As the stage descended a hill, a masked man suddenly jumped out in front of the horses, stopping the coach. "Throw out the box," he demanded while pointing a shotgun at Charley Seavy, the driver. The masked robber escaped with nearly $400 in coins, a $200 diamond ring, and a $25 watch. But he left behind his second and final poem in the broken treasure box, this one written on brown paper:

Here I lay me down to sleep
to wait the coming morrow
perhaps success perhaps defeat
and everlasting sorrow.
Let come what will I'll try it on
my condition can't be worse
and if there's money in that box
tis munny [sic] in my purse.

Black Bart the Po8

Agents WILL PRESERVE a copy on file in their office.

$800.00 Reward!

ARREST STAGE ROBBER!

1.

On the 3d of August, 1877, the stage from Fort Ross to Russian River was stopped by one man, who took from the Express box about $300, coin, and a check for $305.52, on Grangers' Bank of San Francisco, in favor of Fisk Bros. The Mail was also robbed. On one of the Way Bills left with the box the Robber wrote as follows:—

> "I've labored long and hard for bread—
> For honor and for riches—
> But on my corns too long you've trod,
> You fine haired sons of bitches.
> BLACK BART, the P o 8.

Driver, give my respects to our friend, the other driver; but I really had a notion to hang my old disguise hat on his weather eye." (fac simile.)

It is believed that he went to the Town of Guerneville about daylight next morning.

2.

About one year after above robbery, July 25th, 1878, the Stage from Quincy to Oroville was stopped by one man, and W., F. & Co's box robbed of $379. coin, one Diamond Ring, (said to be worth $200) one Silver Watch, valued at $25. The Mail was also robbed. In the box, when found next day, was the following, (fac simile):—

Black Bart's poetry is displayed on a reward poster.

After the next robbery a few days later on July 30 in Plumas County, Wells Fargo issued a private circular to Wells Fargo agents and local sheriffs containing a reproduction of the poems in Bart's disguised handwriting and details of his robberies. At the bottom appeared the following: "It will be seen from the above that this fellow is a character that would be remembered as a scribbler and something of a wit or wag, and would be likely to leave specimens of his handwriting on hotel registers and other public places."

Anyone with information was urged to contact Wells Fargo's special officer, James B. Hume. The circular did not remain private for long, and newspapers soon carried information about Bart and his poetry to readers. Soon, everyone was talking about the bandit Po8. A key clue, Bart's upside-down T slashing of the mail bags, was not made public and remained a way to connect him to future robberies.

On October 2 Bart held up the Cahto-to-Ukiah stage, which yielded him $40 and a gold watch. Trackers hired by Wells Fargo followed his escape trail for 60 miles before losing him. Less than two days later, Bart stopped and robbed the stage from Covelo to Ukiah, this time earning $400 for his efforts. On October 4, when Jim Hume arrived on the scene, he discovered peach pits behind a tree on the side of the road—Bart's meal while waiting for the stage. With this robbery, the reward for Bart's capture increased to $800: $300 from Wells Fargo, $300 from the State of California, and $200 from the United States Post Office.

Jim, on horseback, tracked Bart's trail for miles, questioning people along the way. By now, Jim understood that Bart always escaped on foot, but he wondered how the robber could travel long distances so quickly.

It was common, then, for lone travelers to stop at rural farms along their way for a bit of food or to spend the night. These unexpected guests brought welcome news and friendly conversation to isolated farm families. Bart, it appears, took advantage of this hospitality. Jim Hume suspected this and went out of his way to question travelers and homeowners about strangers they encountered after a stage robbery. For Jim, the descriptions of one such guest provided details about the man who was now at the top of Wells Fargo's list of wanted criminals.

After the last robbery, Bart had made his way to the Eel River ranch of the McCreary family. Fourteen-year-old Donna, who served a meal to the stranger, later provided Hume with a specific description. The guest was about 5 feet 8 inches tall, weighed about 160 pounds, with light gray eyes, bushy eyebrows, and two missing front teeth. His black hair was tinged with gray and thinning at the temples. He wore a full mustache and had a mole on his left cheek. Donna noticed that his coat sleeve was slightly torn and mended with white thread. He had split open his shoes with a knife to lighten the pressure on his toes. Donna's mother thought their visitor was a traveling minister and remarked on the man's politeness and conversational ability. He didn't smoke or drink alcohol. But Jim knew who this man was and issued a circular to Wells Fargo agents and law officers with Bart's description, which quickly went public in local newspapers.

No more was heard of Black Bart until the next robbery nine months later on June 21, 1879. By then, he had become a folk hero. His public image was of a polite road agent who never harmed or robbed passengers. His only targets were the Wells Fargo treasure boxes and US Post Office mail bags. Bart told one driver, "Sure hope you have a lot of gold in that strongbox. I'm nearly out of money." Jim Hume now had a new theory about Bart's crime schedule. Black Bart only robbed when he ran out of money. While he was always seen with his double-barreled shotgun, he never fired a shot.

The public interest in Black Bart grew with each succeeding robbery and only intensified Jim Hume's efforts to capture him. Some even thought that Bart had supernatural powers. How else could a robber on foot, without a horse, rob stagecoaches 60 miles apart in mountainous country within 24 hours?

After each new robbery, Jim and law officers tried to track Bart's escape route without much luck. The bandit seemed to simply disappear on foot into the countryside, only to reappear and rob again a distance away. "Detectives on his trail found that after a robbery he never stopped to make camp and cook a meal until twelve or fifteen miles away from the scene of the holdup. Quite a wonderful walker was the man in the linen duster." Two days after robbing the Redding-bound stage on October 25, Bart stopped another stage on October 27, 1879, 35 miles away.

Black Bart and James Hume were engaged in a public battle of wits. During the September 1, 1880, robbery of the Weaverville-to-Redding stage, Bart asked the driver to give regards to Jim Hume. Jim was not amused and intensified his investigation. As Jim interviewed farmers along Bart's escape routes, witnesses confirmed the McCrearys' detailed description of the robber. The next day, on September 2, Jim received a report that a man with Bart's features had stopped at rancher J. T. Adkinson's cabin on Eagle Creek. The man had asked for some food, and the rancher prepared a wrapped lunch, which the stranger gratefully accepted and went on his way. Adkinson's description of his visitor fit Bart, but the rancher could not believe that the polite, friendly man he'd met could be a notorious criminal.

Other mountain people who met Bart had the same opinion. One man remembered, "He was a polite, agreeable man who had told them that he was a miner and that he suffered from a disease of the throat." With similar reports about other sightings, Jim now knew all about Bart's robbery techniques and how the highwayman looked and behaved. What he didn't know was Bart's real identity and where he would strike next.

While Jim was discouraged, Bart also experienced difficult moments. During his robbery of the northbound stage from Roseburg, Oregon, to Redding on November 20, 1880, driver Joe Morgan threw down the mail sacks but told Bart the treasure box was too heavy to lift. Bart, his shotgun at the ready, climbed on the wheel to help lift the box. Just then, Morgan reached for a hatchet hidden under his seat and swung at the robber, just missing his head. Bart, frightened by this unexpected turn of events, dropped away quickly, leaving the box untouched. A newspaper wrongly suggested, "The robber was probably a green hand." But Black Bart was no amateur.

There was at least one other close call for Bart. At a small country hotel, a stagecoach driver thought he recognized the man who had held him up. He whispered his suspicion to the landlord, who responded, "Why, man, you're crazy. . . . I know he was in his room after the stage went by, because he called the porter up." But he wasn't. As the stage passed the hotel, Bart did call the porter to his room, then after the porter left he slipped unnoticed out of the house. Bart paddled across the river in a small boat in time to overtake and rob the stage. He then returned unnoticed to the hotel and "sauntered down from his room to breakfast just as the stage driver came in with his tale of a desperate highwayman."

Jim devised ways to make Bart's life more difficult. First, realizing that Bart only stopped stages that did not have shotgun messengers, Jim added armed guards to an increasing number of stagecoach runs, particularly those carrying large amounts of gold and money. He also ordered more of the Wells Fargo treasure boxes to be chained down inside the coaches. When Bart encountered his first such box on August 31, 1881, he ordered the driver, John Sulloway, to get off the coach and hold the horses while he climbed in and smashed the box open with his ax.

Jim Hume got another clue about the timing of Bart's robberies. Horace Williams, driver of the Yreka-to-Redding stage on October 8, 1881, asked Bart, "How do you make it anyway?" Bart responded, "I don't make it very well for the chances I have to take." It seems that in some robberies, Bart did not find much money but in others he did. It was hard and dangerous work. Wells Fargo was often not forthcoming in publicizing the amounts robbers took from their treasure boxes.

Bart's reputation for politeness was sometimes not deserved. In his robbing of the Lakeview-to-Redding stage on October 11, 1881, an unusually nervous Bart acted especially crude, leading some to believe that it was not really him but a copycat. He threatened the driver to throw down the box or "I'll blow your head off!" Then, unlike in his previous robberies, he pointed his gun at the passengers in the coach. After he ordered the stage to move on, a scared young boy riding next to the driver said, "I'm glad the robber didn't get my parcel." When the driver asked him what was inside, the boy answered, "I've got my lunch in it." Later, referring to the small amount of money Bart got in that robbery, Jim Hume said, "That stage robber would have been better off if he'd left the Wells Fargo box and taken the kid's lunch."

While the robberies continued to perplex Jim Hume, ordinary citizens wondered whether Black Bart would ever be caught. One newspaper reflected on the lack of success in tracking him down: "The roads in many parts of Northern California have been troubled a great deal . . . by one-man highway adventures, and the bold man of the road has always escaped capture." Then, perhaps taking a dig at Jim, the article ended with, "Certain it is that the job is one for a good detective." Writing about the standoff between Jim and Bart, another newspaper commented, "If Detective Hume fails to catch him before he dies, he will count his life a blank and his labor wasted."

No one then realized just how close Jim was to solving the puzzle of Black Bart.

5

CLOSING IN

This fellow [Bart] is a character that
will be remembered as a scribbler and
something of a wit and a wag.

—WELLS FARGO REWARD CIRCULAR

The clues Jim Hume discovered about the road
agent's identity and techniques did not bring Wells
Fargo any closer to capturing him. Jim had many cases
to solve, and the pressure of constant travel made him
"dusty, tired, worn-out and ill tempered." On his way
to investigate yet another robbery, his stage was held
up. A newspaper commented, "This method of turning the tables was certainly a bold stroke. The thieves
have particular reason to feel proud, as Mr. Hume is
one of the coolest and bravest men in the State."

During another trip in the Arizona Territory, Jim again found himself on the other side of a gun when two masked men held up the stage he was on, traveling between Contention and Tombstone, Arizona. The stage did not carry a treasure box or mail, but the robbers did take Jim's two fine revolvers and some cash. Wells Fargo offered a reward of $300, but the bandits were never found. One newspaper headline declared, A WELL-KNOWN DETECTIVE FINDS SOME HIGHWAYMEN HE WAS NOT LOOKING FOR.

Bart was not the only stage robber plaguing Wells Fargo, but at least Jim could identify which robberies were Bart's work by the following:

- ☞ The white flour sack over his head had holes cut out for the eyes.
- ☞ Bart crouched in front of the lead horses to avoid being shot.
- ☞ Bart carried a double-barreled shotgun.
- ☞ He always brought an old ax to smash open the treasure box.
- ☞ He cut the US Mail sacks in a unique upside-down T.
- ☞ He was not heard from during the winter months.

In addition, Jim had a very accurate physical description of Bart that he'd pieced together from ordinary people who, like Mrs. McCreary and others, innocently fed and hosted the polite stranger. People who met Bart along the way told Jim that he carried a good-sized blanket roll, which Jim suspected contained a broken-down shotgun. They also gave Jim a detailed description of the clothes Bart wore. He was "dressed in steel-mixed coat and vest, checked wool shirt, blue overalls outside and red duck pants underneath: kip boots badly worn and run over on inside: dirty light-colored felt hat: silver watch and heavy link silver chain."

Jim circulated Bart's description to law officers and Wells Fargo agents in 1880, even providing a name. The wanted robber, the circular stated, was Harry Barton. That was one of the aliases Bart used when he registered in a hotel. The circular duplicated Barton's handwritten signature, which closely matched the writing on Bart's earlier poetry. Jim interviewed rural residents who came in contact with Bart shortly after a robbery. The day after the September 1, 1880, robbery of the Weaverville-to-Redding stage, Bart was at the house of J. T. Adkinson, where he was treated to breakfast and lunch. The next day, Bart was seen on the road by a railroad worker. After a September 16 robbery, Bart was seen in Jacksonville, Oregon. From all

A view of Sonora, California, in gold rush country, where Black Bart robbed.

of these eyewitnesses Jim pieced together a description, which Wells Fargo widely distributed:

Name. Harry Barton: American, of Irish descent: aged 47 years: height, 5 feet 9 or 10 inches: eyes light blue: eyebrows heavy and projecting: hair sandy mixed with gray; whiskers about three inches long, sandy: and grayish on side of face: moustache heavy, sandy and gray: forehead broad and high: features long and cheeks a little sunken: two upper front teeth gone, and one lower front tooth pushed in: tonsils of throat affected from salivation, making a peculiarity of voice: reads with paper at arms length: hands long and bony: third finger of right hand crooked at first joint: shoulders and chest quite stout: lower part of body slender: stands up straight and erect and steps quick and fast when walking.

Bart probably understood that with each robbery, his risk of capture increased. He probably realized too that, despite his disguise, more people now were aware of his description. One close call happened on July 13, 1882, when Bart, for the first time, chose to rob a stage guarded by an armed Wells Fargo messenger.

There were not enough messengers available to accompany all stages, so Wells Fargo assigned messengers only to stages carrying a large amount of gold or cash. As the stage traveled along level ground near La Porte, veteran driver Hank Helm was surprised by a man who ran out into the road and crouched to grab at the lead horses. "He wore a linen duster," he recalled, "and his face was covered with a big, white mask. I whooped up the horses with a view to get past him." But the frightened team instead came to a stop. George Hackett, the shotgun messenger, raised his weapon and fired at the robber. The blast blew off the road agent's hat and grazed his head. The robber then "ran down the hill, straight away from the road," with Hackett in pursuit on foot into the brush.

Unable to catch up to the robber, who "dodged from tree to tree, and finally escaped," Hackett made his way back to the stage. He picked up the hat blown off the robber's head and later gave a description: "It was a soft hat of black felt, very old and weather-beaten, and full of ragged rents. It had four fresh buck-shot holes in it, with hair sticking to some of them." Next to the hat was the bloodied white mask, with a hole shot through it. In his haste to flee, Bart left behind two small binoculars. The authorities were notified, and "parties were immediately started in pursuit, who expect to soon find their man, either dead or badly wounded."

Did Bart choose this stage at random, or did he know that the guarded treasure box contained $18,000, which made it worth the risk? Jim, close on the trail but still unable to capture Bart, now had a few more clues to add to his list.

Apparently, Bart recovered quickly from his wound and next stopped the Yreka-to-Redding stage on September 17, 1882. After ordering the passengers out of the stage and telling them to go ahead a distance on foot, Bart had the driver leave his seat and drop to the ground to take hold of the horses. Meanwhile, Bart climbed up and broke the box. The driver asked Bart, "This is a nice night, isn't it . . . are you getting anything?" Bart's response was "Not much." One report later said the box contained only 35 cents!

Bart's last robbery in 1882 was on November 24 when he held up the Lakeport-to-Cloverdale stage. No more was heard of him until April 12, 1883, when he robbed the same stage again and carried away two express boxes and six mail sacks. On June 23, Bart robbed the Jackson-to-Ione stage, stealing $750 and the contents of the mail sacks. The *Chico Record* newspaper reported that "J.B. Hume is on the trail of Black Bart, the daring road agent," but then, with a bit of humor, commented,

"That is probably about as close to Black Bart as Hume will ever get." Continued frustration did not stop Jim's relentless pursuit. He continued to interview rural residents after each robbery and used that information to add more details to his description of the robber.

In a circular sent to law officers on December 18, 1882, Jim provided new information about Bart gathered through his continuing investigations:

Wells Fargo stagecoaches offered scheduled trips throughout the West.

He is polite to all passengers, and especially so
to ladies. He comes and goes from the scene of
robbery on foot; seems to be a thorough moun-
taineer, and a good walker, as he sometimes
covers long distances in a day—getting food
from houses in out-of-the way places, but has
never been known to remain over night in a
house that is occupied; never allows himself to
be seen in the vicinity of robbery, and never
seeks food until 12 or 15 miles away. . . . It is
not believed that he is addicted to the use of
liquor and tobacco; is a great lover of coffee,
wears about a No. 8 boot; is a great reader and,
when reading without glasses, holds his paper
off at full arm's length.

Black Bart stood out from other stagecoach robbers
of his time. One newspaper commented, "There are
very few 'Black Barts' among the road agents Captain
Hume has to deal with. Few of them are gentlemanly
and mild mannered, as Black Bart is described. Most of
the characters . . . are quite as willing to take a life as
make the request, 'Throw down that box!'"

But Jim Hume was determined to catch Bart, gentlemanly or not. On September 5, 1883, Jim issued
detailed orders to all Wells Fargo agents about the

immediate actions they needed to take after any future Bart holdup. The information indicates how advanced Jim had become in organizing a fast but professional response to a Black Bart robbery.

> Hereafter, should the stage to your place be robbed by one man, I desire you to IMMEDI-ATELY send two competent persons to scene of robbery, instructed to gather up box, mail bags (if taken) and everything that they may find in way of disguises, tools, etc. and one to hasten back and report, the other to stay on the ground taking measurement of all tracks and noticing and noting everything that may tend to bear in any way upon the robbery, or aid in pursuit by those who follow.

In addition, Jim ordered local agents to organize "proper persons in your community, who will at all time be prepared with arms, etc, for quick work, when required." He urged them to not only track the robber and try to overtake him but also telegraph ahead to law officers in the direction of the escape. Finally, Jim told agents to continue publicizing the $800 reward for Bart's arrest and conviction. Knowing he could not track Bart alone, Jim drew on other law professionals for help. His immediate assistant was Wells Fargo special officer John N. Thacker, who was hired in 1875. Charles Aull, the San Quentin warden and Jim's close friend, was appointed a temporary Wells Fargo detective.

Although Jim had no idea where or when Bart would strike next, the Wells Fargo chief detective was tightening a noose around the elusive robber.

6

THE CAPTURE

A ten-year-old could have captured me.

—BLACK BART

Sometimes returning to the scene of the crime can be a bad idea. On November 3, 1883, Black Bart decided to rob the Sonora-to-Milton stage again, at Funk Hill, the same spot of his first robbery. After 27 successful robberies, perhaps he was overconfident. The ghostlike figure wore a flour sack over his head, with two holes for his eyes, topped by a derby hat. He held a shotgun aimed at the driver. "Throw down that box," he ordered.

"I can't," driver Reason McConnell, answered.

This time, the box was bolted to the floor inside the stage. Bart ordered McConnell to unhitch the horses and move ahead with them, away from the stage. As Bart climbed into the coach, he was relieved to see it empty of people. Unfortunately for him, he did not see the passenger who was not there.

Bart got to work on the treasure box, which was bound with iron. It was hard work. It took him nearly half an hour to break. But he must have been pleased with this haul, which contained 228 ounces of gold worth $4,400, some gold dust, and coins. Bart quickly gathered up the riches and bid McConnell goodbye. He then set off into the brush with his shotgun under his right arm.

Jimmy Rolleri was a local teenager who liked to hunt. Earlier that day he had decided to ride along with the stagecoach driver and try his luck at hunting. Before the stage began the slow climb up Funk Hill, Jimmy got off with his rifle. His plan was to scout the area for game and rejoin the slow-moving stage on the other side. As Black Bart made his escape, McConnell caught sight of Jimmy and signaled him to quietly bring the rifle. The driver took the weapon and fired at the escaping robber.

The first shot surprised the bandit. A second shot convinced him to run. Neither shot hit him. "Here. Give it here. I won't miss," Jimmy said, and grabbed the rifle back from McConnell. The teenager's shot struck the bandit's hand, leaving a trail of stolen mail and blood as Bart fled. Black Bart later said, "A ten-year-old could have captured me."

Reason McConnell rehitched the horses and hurried off into Copperopolis, the nearest town, where he notified the authorities. A posse formed and headed out to the site of the robbery with Calaveras County Sheriff Ben Thorn. Jim Hume was notified, and while he headed to the scene, the sheriff collected evidence. Thorn then set off to track Bart, notifying neighboring sheriffs Tom Cunningham of San Joaquin County and George McQuade of Tuolumne County to be on the lookout. On the road, Thorn interviewed a trapper, Thomas Martin, who identified a man who'd stopped at his cabin for food and fit the robber's description.

This time, the robber left behind a long-awaited abundance of clues for Jim Hume: a derby hat, empty flour sack masks, a bag of crackers, and a handkerchief. When Jim examined the handkerchief he noticed faded letters and a number etched into the cloth—F.X.O.7—a laundry mark. Jim knew that laundries marked clothing with a special code by which to identify each customer. When he found the customer who belonged to that mark, he would finally find Black Bart.

Jim returned to San Francisco and handed the handkerchief to Harry Morse, a former sheriff who had established his own detective agency in the city. Morse set out to visit all 91 laundries in San Francisco. Jim had long theorized that Bart lived there and used the city as his headquarters between holdups.

For eight days Morse trudged from one laundry to the next until he finally traced the mark to a small tobacco shop and laundry agency at 316 Bush Street, owned by Thomas Ware. The helpful shopkeeper identified the laundry mark as belonging to C. E. Bolton, a mining engineer who regularly brought his laundry to the shop. Ware offered to introduce Morse to the handkerchief's owner. Morse discovered that Bolton lived in room 40 of the Webb House, located at 37 Second Street, and stationed a plainclothes detective outside to watch for Bolton. When Bolton did not appear, Morse returned to Ware's shop. By chance, Ware saw Bolton approaching. In a matter of minutes, Ware introduced Bolton to Morse, who found himself standing before a man who "was elegantly dressed, carried a cane, wore a natty little derby hat, a diamond pin, a large diamond ring on his little finger and heavy gold watch and chain."

"He looked anything but a robber," Morse later said, "[but] I knew he was the man I wanted." Thanks to Jim Hume's detailed detective work, Morse "knew at once from the description and his hollow voice that the fellow was Black Bart." He thought quickly and invited

Bolton to walk along with him to discuss a mining opportunity.

Morse guided the well-dressed man to a building at 320 Sansome Street and up the stairs to the second-floor offices of Wells, Fargo & Company. Bolton seemed unconcerned. With a twinkle in his eye, Morse took great pleasure in introducing Charles Bolton to James Hume. After eight years, the search for Black Bart, the Po8 bandit, was over.

Bolton at first denied that he was Black Bart. When Hume pointed to the F.X.O.7 mark, Bolton said, "Why someone may have stolen the handkerchief from me." Hume asked Bolton to put on the derby hat found at the robbery scene.

"Why, gentlemen," Bolton said, "it fits very well, doesn't it? And it's a very good hat. Perhaps you would allow me to buy it?"

As Hume's questioning continued, Bolton angrily exclaimed, "I am a gentleman. I do not know either of you, nor in what way my personal business concerns you." Morse, remembering the bloody waybill left at the scene of the robbery, observed that Bolton's right hand showed fresh healing.

"How did you receive that wound?" he asked.

Bolton responded, "It is none of your business, but I will tell you. I struck it on the car rail at Reno."

San Francisco offices of Wells Fargo.

"No you didn't," Morse responded, "you got it when you broke open Wells, Fargo's box."

Bolton was silent. Hume and Morse then called in Captain Appleton W. Stone of the San Francisco Police, who placed Bolton under arrest. Then the three officers accompanied him to his home.

A thorough search of Bolton's apartment revealed other handkerchiefs carrying the same laundry mark. Morse again showed Bolton the handkerchief found at the robbery site and reminded him, "It was found where you dropped it after robbing the Sonora stage."

Bolton responded, "I am certainly not the only individual with this laundry mark on his clothes." At that point, Bolton became angry and blurted, "What! Do you take me for a stage robber? This is the first time my character has been brought into question," and threatened to sue Wells Fargo.

Hanging in the room was a set of old clothes identified as those worn by Bart at the last holdup. A Bible was also found with an inscription: TO MY BELOVED HUSBAND, CHARLES E. BOLES, finally revealing his real name.

As Hume, Morse, and Stone escorted Boles back down the stairs, they encountered the landlady. Ever the gentleman, Boles told her that he was suddenly called away on business by his three friends. He offered to pay his rent right then and there but could only

Charles E. Boles,
alias Black Bart, alias
Charles Bolton, shortly
after his capture.

offer gold coins for
which she did not have
change. Morse then
took a dollar from his
own pocket and gave
it to the landlady. With
his rent fully paid up,
Boles spent the night
in the San Francisco
City Jail.

The next day a
reporter went to the
rooming house and
asked the landlady if Charles Bolton lived there. She
innocently replied, "Yes, he does. Can you tell me where
he is? He went away very mysteriously last night." Upon
hearing that her respected lodger was Black Bart, she

The lawmen who helped capture Black Bart. Seated left to right: Tom Cunningham, Ben Thorn, Harry Morse. Standing left to right: A. W. Stone, John Thacker.

responded, "Oh, my! That man a stage robber! Who would have thought it? Why, he told me that he was a mining man." Then she nearly fainted.

From all accounts, Bolton was a good neighbor. He enjoyed reading and even spent time writing poetry. He had a hobby—painting watercolors. He was a good card player and often went to the theater after dinner. He never received or sent mail but enjoyed reading the daily newspapers.

The next morning, Morse, John Thacker of Wells Fargo, and Captain Stone of the San Francisco Police took Boles to San Andreas, to be charged in Calaveras County, where the robbery took place. There, Thomas Martin, the eyewitness who had seen Boles in the area at the time of the robbery, would identify him. During the trip, the outwardly calm robber refused to admit to the crime.

News of the arrest spread quickly, and a large crowd of curious onlookers greeted Boles upon his arrival. After dinner, Morse took Boles into a room and began interrogating him about the robbery. He presented Boles with all the evidence that had been collected and urged him to confess. Boles refused at first but eventually told Morse, "I don't admit that I did this, but what would happen to the man who did—if he should confess?"

Morse told him that such a confession would earn the criminal a lighter jail sentence. Boles then confessed and offered Morse a surprising bit of information—the shotgun he carried was never loaded.

Boles also volunteered to show where he had hidden the treasure taken during the last robbery. That night, Boles, accompanied by Morse, Stone, and Sheriff Thorn of Calaveras County, rode 24 miles away near the scene of the robbery and pointed out where the loot was hidden. The next day, Morse sent the following message to Wells Fargo: "'Black Bart' throws up the sponge. Stone, Thorne and myself have recovered all the stolen treasure."

Wells Fargo arranged visits for Black Bart to several photography shops, and his portraits soon appeared in newspapers and on souvenir postcards. The photos were very popular in San Francisco and the areas of Bart's successful holdups. Everyone wanted to see what the legendary masked bandit looked like. Many were surprised to see the photograph of a well-dressed, prosperous-looking gentleman staring back at them. He did not fit the image of the typical stage robber. But his appearance perfectly fit the description Jim Hume publicized in 1878 of Bart's visit with the McCreary family.

Boles provided the law officers with a detailed description of his escape after the last robbery. After hastily hiding the treasure in a hollowed-out log, he walked 100 miles, eventually arriving in Brighton, near Sacramento, 50 hours later. Dressed in a new change of clothes he bought in Sacramento, he made his way by train to Reno, Nevada, where he spent a few days. Then it was back to San Francisco, where, to be safe, he stayed overnight in a hotel. Then he returned to his lodgings and resumed his usual city life.

Police officers were surprised to later learn that, when in San Francisco, Boles often took his meals in the New York Bakery, a Kearney Street restaurant frequented by them. They could not believe that the well-dressed model gentleman, a polite mining engineer with whom they had had many pleasant conversations, was a wanted criminal.

Judge C. V. Gottschalk of Calaveras County sentenced Charles E. Boles, also known as Charles E. Bolton and Black Bart, to six years in San Quentin Prison. Boles admitted to only the one robbery and implored the judge for mercy. When asked if he denied he was Black Bart, he replied, "The officers say that I am Bart, though I say not." Jim Hume was convinced otherwise since Boles actually confessed to him that he really committed all the robberies but only publicly accepted responsibility for the last one. On behalf of Wells Fargo, Jim issued a circular stating that "all doubts are at rest—that the man is really the notorious highwayman 'Black Bart, the Po8.'" Appended to the announcement was a list of Bart's 28 robberies. A newspaper reported that Boles "seemed rather pleased with the sentence."

For his part in capturing the robber, Wells Fargo presented Jimmy Rolleri with a specially designed rifle. Detective Morse and the other officers split the $800 reward and one-quarter of the recovered money. Hume and Thacker, as Wells Fargo employees, received their regular salaries and did not share in the reward money.

Sheriff Thorn accompanied the now convicted robber by train back to San Francisco to serve his jail sentence. Awaiting them was a crowd of well-wishers. The *San Francisco Chronicle* commented that if the Po8 Bandit had been the famous poet Henry Wadsworth Longfellow, the reception could not have been better. On the way to San Quentin Prison, Boles was greeted by old friends. William Pike of the New York Bakery was there, and when Thomas Ware, the laundry owner, tried to convey his sorrow for identifying him, Boles turned to him and said, "I know that my dear fellow. Don't talk about it any more." Even his landlady came to wish him well. With tears rolling down her cheeks, she spoke softly and left him with a simple "Good-bye."

(Agents of WELLS, FARGO & CO. will please place this in the hands of local Officers and Business Men and preserve a copy in Office. ☞ DO NOT POST. ☜)

ARREST STAGE ROBBER.

LIBERAL REWARD.

The Stage from Sonora to Milton, Cal., was stopped by one man Saturday morning, the 3d inst., about three miles east of Copperopolis, and Wells, Fargo & Co's Express robbed of $4,700 in treasure, described as follows:

One cake of retorted gold amalgam of a conical shape, 5½ inches in width across the top, 5½ inches in depth; of a rich yellow color; weight 228 ozs.; fineness 874, and assay value $18 per oz.

One parcel gold dust 3¼ oz. fineness and value unknown.

Several parcels coin $553, mostly gold.

In addition to the *standing reward* of $300, offered by the State for the arrest and conviction of each such offender, Wells, Fargo & Co. have a like *standing reward* on same terms, and will also give one-fourth of any treasure recovered.

Gold Dust buyers, Bankers and Assayers are especially requested to keep a sharp lookout. Any person giving the undersigned, information that leads to the arrest and conviction of robber or recovery of treasure will be suitably rewarded.

JAMES B. HUME,

Special Officer W. F. & Co.

San Francisco, No. 5, 1883.

Wells Fargo's announcement of Black Bart's last robbery.

San Quentin Prison.

When asked why he returned to the same robbery site after eight years, Boles told Hume, "It still was the best holdup spot on the road." To a reporter, he said, "If I had my usual time to clean up and cover my tracks they never would have caught me and they never would have found the 'stuff.'"

By all accounts, Bart was a model prisoner. He obeyed the prison rules and largely kept to himself with limited interaction with others. After little more than four years in jail, Black Bart, prisoner number 11046, was released early for good behavior, on February 23, 1888. A reporter asked if he planned on robbing any more stagecoaches. He answered no. When asked if he planned to write any more poetry, he smiled and said, "Didn't you just hear me say that I wasn't going to commit any more crimes?"

POEM ABOUT A POET

———•———

The saga of Black Bart did not disappear with his imprisonment. Stories about his exploits continued to circulate, some true but most not. Famed writer Ambrose Bierce wrote a witty poem called "Black Bart, Po8" originally published in the *San Francisco Examiner* on January 29, 1888, a few weeks before Bart's release from San Quentin. It began with these lines:

*Welcome, good friend; as you have served
    your term,
And found the joy of crime to be a fiction,
I hope you'll hold your present faith, stand
    firm
And not again be open to conviction.*

*Your sins, though scarlet once, are now as
    wool:
You've made atonement for all past
    offences,
And conjugated—'twas an awful pull!—
The verb "to pay" in all its moods and
    tenses.*

*You were a dreadful criminal—by Heaven,
I think there never was a man so sinful!*

7

WHO WAS BLACK BART?

He looked anything but a robber.

—HARRY MORSE

During the eight years that Jim Hume pursued Black Bart, little did he realize just how similar their life stories were. Charles E. Boles was born in England in 1829, and his family came to the United States two years later, settling in Upstate New York. Like Jim, Charley grew up on a farm. His childhood was typical, and he became known locally for his athletic ability, especially his wrestling skills. A friend remembered, "He was a young man of excellent habits and greatly esteemed and respected by all who knew him."

Again, like Jim, the lure of the gold rush led him to leave home and seek his fortune in California. Charley, accompanied by two brothers, James and David, began mining along the American River in late 1849. Less than two years later, they returned to New York. After a short stay, Charley returned to California, this time with David and another brother, Robert. Sadly, both David and Robert became ill and died shortly after their arrival. Charley remained and mined gold for another two years before deciding to head home.

On the trip back, he stopped for a while in Decatur, in Macon County, Illinois, where he met and married Mary Johnson in 1854. The young couple settled there and began to raise a family. But the quiet farming life did not suit Charley, and when the Civil War broke out in 1861, he saw an opportunity for adventure. On August 13, 1862, at age 33, he enlisted in the Illinois Volunteers, 116th Infantry Regiment, Company B, composed of Macon County residents. By November 8, the regiment was on its way to Memphis, Tennessee. The men saw action in the fiercest battles throughout the South.

The 116th endured many hardships during the war. During the Battle of Arkansas Post on January 9–11, 1863, Company B sustained very heavy losses. Boles was one of 25 of the company's survivors. After their victory at the Battle of Chattanooga in November

Portrait of Charles E. Boles. Many noticed his similarity to James B. Hume.

1863, Boles and his fellow soldiers experienced a very cold winter. They kept warm marching 25 to 35 miles during the days and then suffered from the cold while camping at night.

During a battle in Dallas, Georgia, at the end of May 1864, he was seriously wounded by a shot that went through his cartridge box, belt, and shirt, inflicting a deep flesh wound on his left side and leaving a significant scar.

While battling his way through the South, Charley was recognized for his bravery, and as the war ended he was promoted to sergeant. His proud wife gave him a Bible, which she inscribed, "This precious Bible is presented to Charles E. Boles, first sergeant, Co. B, 116th Illinois Volunteer Infantry, by his wife as New Year's gift. God gives us heart to which His [illegible words] . . . faith to believe. Decatur, Illinois, 1865."

A fellow Company B soldier Isaac D. Jennings recalled, "The 116th had its share of real fighting through the war, and that means that he was in a good many places that try men's courage. It can not be recalled that he ever shirked a danger." Jennings never suspected Charley "as having in him the making of a desperate highwayman." Another former soldier, John E. Braden, remembered, "We slept in the same tent for many months. Boles was a good soldier. He was brave, hardy, could endure long marches, had few bad habits and was generally liked. He did not use tobacco, never was profane, and I never saw him drinking anything until after we had taken Columbia, S.C. and then he only drank a little wine." Braden also recalled that Charley was "known as a good penman and a man of considerable education."

When the war ended, the 116th was one of the regiments in the May 1865 Grand Review of the Armies, a parade in Washington, DC, before the president of the United States, Andrew Johnson. Charles E. Boles was mustered out of the army with the rank of first sergeant and made his way back to Decatur. During the previous three years, he had easily marched many miles a day, endured countless hardships, and become comfortable sleeping on the bare ground. Once he learned about Charley's military experiences, Jim Hume finally understood how Black Bart could so quickly and easily travel long distances on foot.

Charley returned home to Decatur, Illinois, but didn't stay long. He sold his farm and moved with his wife and children to a nearby town. Then he was off to Montana to seek his riches in mining. His frequent letters home described successes, and in a last letter to his wife in 1869 he promised to return home and bring his family back to Montana. Addressing "My own dear

Charles E. Boles marched in the Grand Review of the Armies in Washington, DC, at the end of the Civil War.

Mary and little ones," Charley wrote that he and a partner were working on a mine claim, and "if it pays reasonably well we will both come home in the fall. . . . I hope you will not blame me if I fail, and do not put it down too strong that I am coming in the fall."

He ended by asking Mary to "kiss all the little ones for me, and tell them papa is aching to get hold of them once more."

He never returned home. Mary feared he was dead, murdered, or captured by Native Americans. With poverty looming, she sold the house and took on a series of low-paying jobs to support herself and her three daughters. She began referring to herself as the Widow Boles. In 1873 Mary and the children moved to Hannibal, Missouri, where she worked as a seamstress.

Meanwhile, Charley went from Montana to Salt Lake City, Utah, where he remained for two years. Eventually, he arrived back in California to resume the mining activity he had left before the Civil War. He surfaced in San Francisco as Charles Bolton, a respectable mining engineer. He enjoyed city life to the fullest. His rooming house acquaintances later described Bolton as a quiet, dignified, and polite professional who disappeared from time to time to check on his mining interests. Only after his capture were those trips connected to the Wells Fargo stagecoach robberies.

The mystery of how Charley assumed the character of Black Bart was revealed when he disclosed that one of his favorite novels was *The Case of Summerfield* by William Henry Rhodes, which was serialized in local newspapers in the early 1870s. The main character was a robber of Wells Fargo stagecoaches whose name just happened to be Black Bart. When he was writing his first poem at the robbery site, Charley remembered that name and created his new identity.

Only after Bart's capture in 1883 did Mary Boles find out what happened to her husband. His arrest was national news, and she was shocked when she read about the inscription in Bart's Bible proving that the famous stagecoach robber was her long-lost Charley. She communicated with law officers in California, who sent her one of Bart's photographs, which she immediately identified as being of her husband. Mary and Bart exchanged letters for a short time while he was in San Quentin. She was ready to accept him back in her life after he was released, but Bart was not interested. He made his intentions clear in a letter to Mary:

> After waking all these days hoping to be able to comply with your wishes and my own most ardent desires I most sincerely regret that I MUST disappoint you. My dear, it is UTTERLY

impossible for me to come now. . . . Although
I am 'Free' and in fair health, I am most mis-
erable. My Dear family I wish you could give
me up for ever & be happy, for I feel I shall be
a burthen [burden] to you as I live no matter
where I am.

Charley's treatment of his family angered Jim Hume,
who told a reporter, "If anything were needed to prove
him a heartless and unmitigated scoundrel his treatment of his wife and children would do so."

On the day of Bart's release from San Quentin in
1888, a journalist, Charles Michelson, interviewed him.
Bart admitted to Michelson, "I have been a stage robber, but I never stole from a man who could not afford
to lose what I got, and I have helped many a poor man
along. I took my chances, but I never harmed anybody,
and I never pointed a loaded gun at a stage in my life."

Michelson exclaimed, "What?"

"Yes, that is true," Bart responded. "My constant
fear was that I would hurt somebody."

After his release, Bart spent a few weeks in a San
Francisco rooming house. No matter where he went,
his fame accompanied him. Jim Hume made sure
of that. Before his prison release, Jim had sent Bart's
description and photograph to law officials throughout

California and Nevada. Bart departed the city in February and made his way to several other towns before ending up in Visalia, California. He left Visalia on February 23, leaving behind a suitcase in the care of the hotel manager, who notified Hume. When Jim opened the suitcase, he discovered "a package of crackers, a package of sugar, bottle of pickles, can of corned beef, can of lunch tongue, can of currant jelly, pound paper of coffee, two pairs of cuffs and two neckties." One of the cuffs carried a familiar laundry mark: F.X.O.7.

For Jim Hume, the suitcase was proof enough that Bart planned to return to his criminal ways. The contents would sustain Bart as he traveled on foot again to scout out robbery sites. Hume put the blame directly on Bart for new stagecoach robberies in 1888, but in truth, there is no proof that Bart was responsible.

From that point, Bart faded from view, but rumors about his whereabouts did not. He was incorrectly blamed for other stagecoach robberies throughout the West. When a reporter asked, "Is it true, Mr. Hume, that Black Bart was in the pay of your company?" Jim answered, "I am astonished at you asking such a question. If it were so don't you think he would have been only too glad to say in this letter to his wife that he was working instead of writing in such a despondent strain?"

Others claimed to have seen him in such far-flung places as New York, Alaska, and Panama. John Thacker, one of Jim Hume's Wells Fargo detectives, insisted that Bart actually boarded a ship headed to Japan. But in reality, no record exists of Charles E. Boles's activities after leaving Visalia, California. Only the Black Bart legend survived.

EPILOGUE

————————⊷⊶————————

Charles E. Boles was born in England in 1829 and came to the United States when he was two years old. His family settled in upper New York State, where he grew up. With news of the California gold rush in 1849, Boles left home to find his fortune. Like other 49ers, he came to realize he would never strike it rich. On his way back to New York he stopped in Decatur, Illinois, where he married, settled, and became a father to three daughters. When the Civil War broke out, Boles enlisted in the Union Army. His army life was hard. He fought bravely in many battles and proved to be an excellent soldier. It was in the army that he learned to walk long distances and adjust to living outdoors, skills that enhanced his later criminal career. After the war, he returned to his family, but the boredom of everyday life soon overtook him and he headed back to the West. He never saw his wife or children again. Why did he become a stagecoach robber? No one really knows. Upon his release from prison, Charles E. Boles, alias Charles E. Bolton and Black Bart, simply disappeared.

———•———

James B. Hume was born in 1827. Like his adversary Black Bart, he grew up in New York State. Also like Bart, he headed West in 1850 to find his fame and fortune in the gold fields of California. Unlike Bart, he never returned to the East. He had varying success as a gold miner, and in 1860 was elected the deputy tax collector of Placerville, California. From there he moved on to several law enforcement positions. He was a marshal, a sheriff, and finally, the chief detective of Wells, Fargo & Company. He was known and respected for using imaginative law enforcement methods to track down criminals, including Black Bart. Hume died in 1904.

LIST OF ROBBERIES
ATTRIBUTED TO BLACK BART

———— ▸◄━▸◄ ————

Listed here are all the robberies attributed to Black Bart. A few may have been committed by copycat bandits, so the real number committed by Bart could actually be between 27 and 29. Jim Hume used the number 28.

1. **JULY 26, 1875**—Stage from Sonora to Milton

2. **DECEMBER 28, 1875**—Stage from North San Juan to Marysville

3. **JUNE 2, 1876**—Stage from Roseburg to Yreka

4. **AUGUST 3, 1877**—Stage from Fort Ross to Duncans Mills

5. **JULY 25, 1878**—Stage from Quincy to Oroville

6. JULY 30, 1878—Stage from La Porte to Oroville (Plumas County)

7. OCTOBER 2, 1878—Stage from Cahto to Ukiah

8. OCTOBER 3, 1878—Stage from Covelo to Ukiah

9. JUNE 21, 1879—Stage from La Porte to Oroville

10. OCTOBER 25, 1879—Stage from Roseburg to Redding

11. OCTOBER 27, 1879—Stage from Alturas to Redding

12. JULY 22, 1880—Stage from Point Arenas to Duncans Mills

13. SEPTEMBER 1, 1880—Stage from Weaverville to Redding

14. SEPTEMBER 16, 1880—Stage from Roseburg to Yreka

15. SEPTEMBER 23, 1880—Stage from Yreka to Roseburg

16. NOVEMBER 20, 1880—Stage from Roseburg to Redding

17. AUGUST 31, 1881—Stage from Roseburg to Redding

18. OCTOBER 8, 1881—Stage from Yreka to Redding

19. OCTOBER 11, 1881—Stage from Lakeview to Redding

20. DECEMBER 15, 1881—Stage from Downieville to Marysville

21. DECEMBER 27, 1881—Stage from San Juan to Smartsville

22. **JANUARY 26, 1882**—Stage from Ukiah to Cloverdale

23. **JUNE 14, 1882**—Stage from Little Lake to Ukiah

24. **JULY 13, 1882**—Stage from La Porte to Oroville

25. **SEPTEMBER 17, 1882**—Stage from Yreka to Redding

26. **NOVEMBER 24, 1882**—Stage from Lakeport to Cloverdale

27. **APRIL 12, 1883**—Stage from Lakeport to Cloverdale

28. **JUNE 23, 1883**—Stage from Jackson to Ione

29. **NOVEMBER 3, 1883**—Stage from Sonora to Milton

NOTES

CHAPTER 1: A GHOST APPEARS

"Horace Greeley went over this road": Twain, *Roughing It*, 161.

"Please throw down the box": Hoeper, *Black Bart*, 2.

"If he makes a move, give him a volley": Hume and Thacker, *Wells, Fargo & Co.*, 43.

"Do you want to get us all killed?": Hoeper, *Black Bart*, 2.

"No, Ma'am": Hume and Thacker, *Wells, Fargo & Co.*, 43.

"That will be about all, boys": Hungerford, *Wells Fargo*, 142.

"Please throw down the box": Hoeper, *Black Bart*, 3.

"REWARD! Wells, Fargo & Co.'s": Wells Fargo History Room, San Francisco, California.

CHAPTER 2: WELLS FARGO CONNECTS THE WEST

"picking gold out of the": Atlantic, July 1911, 166.

"I soon shall be in 'Frisco": Thomas L. James, "Development of the Overland Mail Service," *Cosmopolitan Magazine*, April 1896, 605.

"I am still here": Erastus Granger, letter to the editor, *Hartford (CT) Courant*, May 21, 1849.

"After the period of six months": *Palmyra (MO) Weekly Whig*, February 7, 1850.

"I hope there are none": *Madison Indiana Herald*, January 22, 1851.

"Two real judges": Kelly, *Stroll Through the Diggings*, 32.

"The miner stoops down": Woods, *Sixteen Months*, 51.

"launched in 1852": *National Magazine*, 1910, 414.

"Freight, Parcels, Money": *Sonoma County Journal*, March 6, 1857.

"It seems that private": *Santa Cruz (CA) Weekly Sentinel*, February 16, 1866.

"The most polite": *National Magazine*, 1910, 420.

"O-ho the Wells Fargo Wagon": Copyright Meredith Willson Music.

"Wells Fargo combined": "History of Wells Fargo," www.wellsfargo.com/about/corporate/history.

"The station-keeper up-ended": Twain, *Roughing It*, 42–43.

"a stout leather strap": Charles F. Lummis, "Pioneer Transportation in America," *McClure's Magazine*, November 1905, 88.

"If there is a prettier": Hungerford, *Covered Wagon*, 10.

"crowded together": Gillilan, *Trail Days*, 113.

"Passengers dozing in corners": Frederick, *Ben Holladay*, 85.

"The best seat inside a stagecoach": Fradkin, *Stagecoach*, 42–43.

"the kind of men you can depend": "About Wells Fargo," www.wellsfargo.com/about.

"Stage robbers were plentiful": Henry J. W. Dam, "A Morning with Bret Harte," *McClure's Magazine*, December 1894, 42.

"were hardly worth": Hume and Thacker, *Wells, Fargo & Co.*, 234.

"The huge vehicle swayed": Harte, *Writings of Bret Harte*, 453.

"Come out with your money" and *"You have no business"*: *Santa Cruz (CA) Weekly Sentinel*, July 30, 1864.

"jumped from behind": *Marysville (CA) Daily Appeal*, October 26, 1876.

"We want the box" through *"There is honor"*: *San Francisco Chronicle*, October 27, 1871.

"get the top of his head": *Petaluma (CA) Weekly Argus*, November 26, 1868.

"You can go ahead": *Santa Cruz (CA) Weekly Sentinel*, July 30, 1864.

"The passengers, eighteen in number": *Santa Cruz (CA) Weekly Sentinel*, June 5, 1875.

"*That's the way to do it*": Quincy (CA) *Feather River Bulletin*, September 18, 1875.

CHAPTER 3: JAMES B. HUME, LAWMAN

"*There is no such thing*": Dillon, *Wells, Fargo Detective*, 62.

"*Mr. Hume intends*": Placerville (CA) *Weekly Mountain Democrat*, June 21, 1862.

"*Our city, under the administration*": Dillon, *Wells, Fargo Detective*, 85.

"*We do not want anything*": Dillon, 92.

"*In that capacity*": "James Bunyan Hume Dies at His Home in Berkeley," *San Francisco Call*, May 19, 1904.

"*It was thwarted*": Dillon, *Wells, Fargo Detective*, 121.

"*Rogues, after they came*": "New Appointment," *Sacramento Daily Union*, May 18, 1872.

"*I'll take the job but*": Bill Armantrout, "James Hume—Frontier Manhunter 'Never Forgot,'" *Ukiah (CA) Daily Journal*, January 16, 1974.

"*The Company offers a standing*": Wells, Fargo & Co.'s Express Instructions, 1884.

"*I discovered two different*": Dillon, *Wells, Fargo Detective*, 154.

"*and getting them*": "Highway Robbers Plead Guilty," *Quincy (CA) Feather River Bulletin*, January 8, 1876.

"*He is a terror to*": "On Business," *Quincy (CA) Feather River Bulletin*, December 27, 1879.

"*J.B. Hume, the head*": *Sacramento Record-Union*, September 15, 1880.

"*As the steamer*": "Turned the Tables," *Sacramento Daily Union*, January 22, 1879.

"*I do not think that man*": "Turned the Tables."

"*He doubtless is better pleased*": *Sacramento Daily Record*, May 1, 1884.

"*corps of officers*" and "*The present effort*": "A Grand Haul," *Sacramento Record-Union*, December 8, 1881.

CHAPTER 4: A LEGEND GROWS

"*Hold up your hands*" through "*probably getting mad*": "Another Stage and Express Robbery," *Marysville (CA) Daily Appeal*, December 17, 1875.

"*This job is the work of a professional*": Hoeper, *Black Bart*, 6.

"*showing the prisoners how hopeless*": "Highway Robbers Plead Guilty," *Marysville (CA) Daily Appeal*, December 29, 1875.

"*throw off the box*": "A Bold Highwayman," *Petaluma (CA) Courier*, August 16, 1877.

"*I've labored long and hard*": "Arrest. Stage Robber," Wells Fargo reward circular.

"*Throw out the box*": *Quincy (CA) Feather River Bulletin*, August 3, 1878.

"*Here I lay me down*": "Arrest. Stage Robber."

"*It will be seen from the above*": Wells Fargo circular.

After the last robbery, Bart had made his way: Collins and Levene, *Black Bart*, 80.

"Sure hope you have": "The Story of Charles E. Boles aka Black Bart," www.sptddog.com/sotp/bbpo8.html.

"Detectives on his trail": *Wells Fargo Messenger*, September 1912, 2.

"He was a polite": *Wells Fargo Messenger*, September 1912, 2.

"The robber was probably": "Stage Robbery—Rich Mines—Weather," *Sacramento Daily Union*, November 22, 1880.

"Why, man, you're crazy" and *"sauntered down from his room"*: Charles Michelson, "Stage Robbers of the West," *Munsey's Magazine*, July 1901, 457.

"How do you make it": Dajani, *Black Bart*, 61.

"I'll blow your head off": "Another Stage and Express Robbery," *Marysville (CA) Daily Appeal*, December 17, 1875.

"I'm glad the robber": Dajani, *Black Bart*, 62–63.

"That stage robber": Hoeper, *Black Bart*, 37.

"The roads in many parts": *Santa Cruz (CA) Weekly Sentinel*, October 15, 1881.

"If Detective Hume fails": *Quincy (CA) Feather River Bulletin*, May 12, 1883.

CHAPTER 5: CLOSING IN

"dusty, tired, worn-out": Dillon, *Wells, Fargo Detective*, 165.

"This method of turning": "Knows How It Is Himself," *Sacramento Record-Union*, August 11, 1881.

A WELL-KNOWN DETECTIVE: *Sacramento Record-Union*, January 9, 1882.

"dressed in steel-mixed coat": Wells Fargo circular, October 23, 1880.

"Name. Harry Barton": Wells Fargo circular, October 23, 1880.

"He wore a linen duster" and *"ran down the hill"*: "Halted By a Road Agent," *Cincinnati Enquirer*, August 18, 1882.

"dodged from tree to tree": "Black Bart and Hackett," *Quincy (CA) Feather River Bulletin*, December 8, 1883.

"It was a soft hat": *Sacramento Daily Union*, July 14, 1882.

"parties were immediately": "Attempted Stage Robbery— Plucky Express Messenger," *Sacramento Daily Union*, July 14, 1882.

"This is a nice night": Dejani, *Black Bart*, 72.

"J.B. Hume is on the trail": *Petaluma (CA) Courier*, January 3, 1883.

"He is polite": *Ukiah (CA) Republican Press*, December 30, 1925.

"There are very few 'Black Barts'": "Science of Stage Robbery," *Pittsburgh Press*, February 4, 1893.

"Hereafter, should the stage" and *"proper persons in your community"*: Wells Fargo circular, September 5, 1883.

CHAPTER 6: THE CAPTURE

"Throw down that box" and *"I can't"*: "Black Bart Caught," *San Francisco Chronicle*, November 14, 1883.

"*Here. Give it here*": Hoeper, *Black Bart*, 66.

"*A ten-year-old*": *San Francisco People's Press*, December 27, 1883.

"*was elegantly dressed*": Hungerford, *Wells Fargo*, 140

"*He looked anything but a robber*": Jackson, *Bad Company*, 154.

"*knew at once*" through "*I am certainly not the only*": John A. Henshall, "Tales of the Early California Bandits III—Black Bart," *Overland Monthly*, June 1909, 478–480.

"*What! Do you take me for*": *Oakland (CA) Tribune*, February 19, 1922.

"*Yes, he does*": "Black Bart Caught," *San Francisco Chronicle*, November 14, 1883.

"*Oh, my! That man a stage robber*": "Black Bart. The Noted Stage Robber Captured at Last," *San Francisco Daily Alta California*, November 14, 1883.

"*I don't admit*": Henshall, "California Bandits," 481.

"*'Black Bart' throws up the sponge*": "Black Bart," *Los Angeles Times*, November 16, 1883.

"*The officers say I am*": "The Poet Robber," *San Francisco Chronicle*, November 20, 1883.

"*all doubts are at rest*": *Sacramento Daily Union*, November 30, 1883.

"*seemed rather pleased*": Jackson, *Bad Company*, 178.

"*I know that*" through "*If I had my usual*": "The Poet Robber," *San Francisco Chronicle*, November 20, 1883.

"Didn't you just hear me say": Frederick (MD) Post, March 22, 1911.

"Welcome, good friend": Bierce, *Collected Works*, 186.

CHAPTER 7: WHO WAS BLACK BART?

"He was a young man": San Francisco Chronicle, January 6, 1884.

"This precious Bible": "The Saga of 'Black Bart,'" *Decatur (IL) Daily Review*, March 3, 1949.

"The 116th had" and *"as having in him"*: "Scrap Basket," *Decatur (IL) Daily Review*, October 26, 1910.

"We slept in the same" and *"known as a good penman"*: "At Highway Robbery," *Decatur (IL) Herald*, December 9, 1888.

"My own dear Mary": "More About Boles," *San Francisco Chronicle*, December 12, 1888.

"After waking all these days" and *"If anything were needed"*: "A Model Husband," *San Francisco Chronicle*, December 11, 1888.

"I have been": Charles Michelson, "Stage Robbers of the West," *Munsey's Magazine*, July 1901, 458.

"a package of crackers": "Bold Black Bart," *San Francisco Chronicle*, November 28, 1888.

"Is it true, Mr. Hume": "More About Boles."

BIBLIOGRAPHY

BOOKS

Bierce, Ambrose. *The Collected Works of Ambrose Bierce.* Vol. 5. New York: Negle, 1911.

Collins, William, and Bruce Levene. *Black Bart: The True Story of the West's Most Famous Stagecoach Robber.* Mendocino, CA: Pacific Transcriptions, 1992.

Dajani, Laika. *Black Bart: Elusive Highwayman-Poet.* Manhattan, KS: Sunflower University Press, 1996.

Dillon, Richard. *Wells, Fargo Detective: A Biography of James B. Hume.* Reno: University of Nevada Press, 1986.

Fradkin, Philip. *Stagecoach: Wells Fargo and the American West.* New York: Simon and Schuster, 2002.

Frederick, James Vincent. *Ben Holladay: The Stagecoach King.* Glendale, CA: Arthur H. Clark, 1940.

Gillilan, James David. *Trail Days*. New York: Abingdon, 1915.

Harte, Bret. *The Writings of Bret Harte*. Boston: Houghton Mifflin, 1896.

Hoeper, George. *Black Bart: Boulevardier Bandit*. Fresno, CA: Word Dancer, 1995.

Hume, James, and John Thacker. *Wells, Fargo & Co. Stagecoach and Train Robberies 1870–1884*. Rev. ed. Jefferson, NC: McFarland, 2010.

Hungerford, Edward. *From Covered Wagon to Streamliner*. New York: Greystone, 1941.

Hungerford, Edward. *Wells Fargo: Advancing the American Frontier*. New York: Bonanza Books, 1949.

Jackson, Joseph Henry. *Bad Company*. Lincoln: University of Nebraska Press, 1977.

Kelly, William. *A Stroll Through the Diggings of California*. Oakland, CA: Biobooks, 1950.

Loomis, Noel. *Wells Fargo: An Illustrated History*. New York: Bramhall House, 1963.

Twain, Mark. *Roughing It*. New York: Harper and Brothers, 1913.

Wilson, Neill. *Treasure Express: The Epic Days of Wells Fargo*. New York: Macmillan, 1936.

Woods, Daniel B. *Sixteen Months at the Gold Diggings*. New York: Harper and Brothers, 1852.

NEWSPAPERS

Cincinnati Enquirer

Decatur (IL) Daily Review

Decatur (IL) Herald

Frederick (MD) Post

Hartford (CT) Courant

Los Angeles Times

Madison Indiana Herald

Marysville (CA) Daily Appeal

Oakland (CA) Tribune

Palmyra (MO) Weekly Whig

Petaluma (CA) Courier

Petaluma (CA) Weekly Argus

Pittsburgh Press

Placerville (CA) Weekly Mountain Democrat

Quincy (CA) Feather River Bulletin

Sacramento Daily Record

Sacramento Daily Union

Sacramento Record-Union

San Francisco Call

San Francisco Chronicle

San Francisco Daily Alta

San Francisco People's Press

Santa Cruz (CA) Weekly Sentinel

Sonoma County (CA) Journal
Ukiah (CA) Daily Journal
Ukiah (CA) Republican Press

PERIODICALS

Atlantic
Cosmopolitan Magazine
McClure's Magazine
Munsey's Magazine
National Magazine
Overland Monthly
Wells Fargo Messenger

WEBSITES

www.blackbart.com
www.sptddog.com
www.wellsfargo.com
www.wellsfargohistory.com

IMAGE CREDITS

Page 16–17: Courtesy of the California History Room, California State Library, Sacramento, California (001383475)

Page 18: Photos used with permission from Wells Fargo Bank, NA

Page 20: Photo used with permission from Wells Fargo Bank, NA

Page 22: Library of Congress (LC-DIG-ds-04481)

Page 23: Photo used with permission from Wells Fargo Bank, NA

Page 24–25: Courtesy of the California History Room, California State Library, Sacramento, California (001528951)

Page 26–27: Courtesy of the California History Room, California State Library, Sacramento, California (001389341)

Page 40: Photo used with permission from Wells Fargo Bank, NA

Page 40: Photo used with permission from Wells Fargo Bank, NA

Page 44: Photo used with permission from Wells Fargo Bank, NA

Page 45: Library of Congress (LC-USZ62-72001)

Page 48–49: Courtesy of the California History Room, California State Library, Sacramento, California (001378519)

Page 53: Photo used with permission from Wells Fargo Bank, NA

Page 58–59: Photo used with permission from Wells Fargo Bank, NA (6542-7)

Page 64–65: Courtesy of the California State History Room, California State Library, Sacramento, California (001394541)

Page 68–69: Courtesy of the California History Room, California State Library, Sacramento, California (001431583)

Page 71: Photo used with permission from Wells Fargo Bank, NA

Page 84–85: Library of Congress (LC-DIG-ppmsca-32167)

Page 89: Photo used with permission from Wells Fargo Bank, NA (300.2011.291)

Page 98–99: Photo used with permission from Wells Fargo Bank, NA

Page 101: Photo used with permission from Wells Fargo Bank, NA

Page 102: Photo used with permission from Wells Fargo Bank, NA

Page 107: Photo used with permission from Wells Fargo Bank, NA

Page 108–9: Courtesy of the California History Room, California State Library, Sacramento, California

Page 115: Photo used with permission from Wells Fargo Bank, NA

Page 118–19: Library of Congress (32217u)

INDEX

———————